THE ART OF PARENTING AN AUTISTIC CHILD

A Complete Guide to Navigating ASD, Early Intervention, and Positive Family Dynamics for Optimal Child Development

CARMEN M. ROBERTS

The Author of the Fight of her Life

Copyright © by Carmen M. Roberts 2023.

Written by: Carmen M. Roberts

This book is designed to provide accurate and Authoritative information in regard to the subject matter covered. If expert assistance or counseling are needed, the service of a component professional should be sought.

In the paperback and hardcover editions of this book, you'll find and added bonus: A complimentary 20-page journal to help you document milestones you achieved as you embark on this journey.

Contents

INTRODUCTION

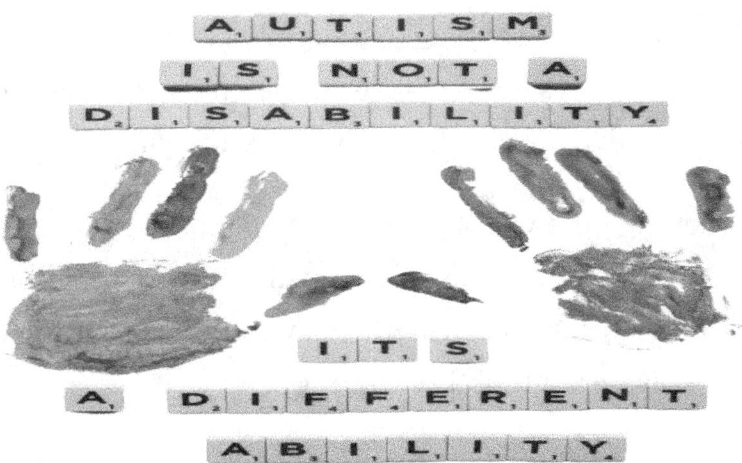

In the peaceful nooks and crannies of suburban life, where people smile at one another and children's laughter fills the air, I discovered that I was a reluctant passenger on an adventure that defied the norm. The often-jolly and innocent picture of parenthood took an unexpected turn when my son Oliver was diagnosed with autism spectrum disorder (ASD).

In a society where autism is frequently shrouded in misinformation, our family set out to tell the story of resiliency, growth, and the remarkable beauty that was shown inside the spectrum.

Before Oliver, myths and societal rumors shaped my knowledge of autism. It was a far-off idea, frequently cloaked in ignorance, and my perspective reflected the limited perspective that many others had of it. Oliver's diagnosis was necessary to shatter those preconceptions and inspire a fresh viewpoint.

A flurry of emotions swept through me as the doctor's words, which disclosed Oliver's autism spectrum condition, lingered in the air. After the first shock and panic subsided, a fierce desire emerged to rethink family dynamics, parenthood, and our role as advocates for our exceptional boy.

Oliver started adding his own colors to the world in a very special way. His preoccupation with the soft rustle of leaves, his careful toy placement, and the way he would lose himself in the patterns of sunshine streaming through the window were all subtle beginnings.

He seemed to have a hidden language, a silent symphony that only those who were open to hearing could understand.

It turned into an adventure to navigate these hazy, unsure early days. Oliver's environment was no longer shaped by social conventions; instead, it was a blank canvas ready to be painted with his own color scheme.

Every day brought new surprises: a fresh gesture, a smile shared by two people, and the realization that neurodiversity wasn't abnormal but rather something to be celebrated.

But in the midst of the chuckles and the faint strains of Oliver's own song, a dilemma developed. The worried doctor's remarks reverberated across the clean walls. Oliver's once-promising progress appeared to have stopped. The uncertainty weighed heavily on the air, and clouds of doubt began to collect like storm clouds.

I found myself at a fork in the path during that dire period. The doctors gave a gloomy impression, their brows wrinkled and their eyes kind. However, I was unable to concede defeat as a parent. Like a strong flame, the flicker of hope pushed me to look further.

Equipped with resolute determination, I fully engaged in the realm of research. The illumination of the computer screen became a companion during late evenings, bringing with it research, anecdotes, and tales of families who had weathered comparable storms. Among the studies, one in particular stood out as a beacon of hope that showed the way ahead.

The research evolved into a lifeline rather than just a repository of information. It strengthened a newfound conviction that Oliver's course could be changed with the correct help, encouragement, and unconditional love.

The next few months turned into a purpose-driven painting on a canvas. The research's strategies found their way into our everyday lives. Customized therapies for Oliver's specific requirements served as the paintbrushes with which we painted a future full of opportunities.

The changes were first subtle: more involvement, a moment of connection shared, and the appearance of newly acquired abilities. The symphony that had been silent for a while began to play again with more energy. Once again, Oliver's voyage found its rhythm, and the storm clouds started to part.

Anticipation permeated the room three months later as we sat in the comfortable space filled with medical charts. The doctor, who had before given dire predictions, now entered with a mixture of amazement and curiosity. Oliver, our story's protagonist, was in front of them; he represented tenacity, advancement, and the remarkable potential hidden inside the spectrum.

The doctor's stunned gaze expanded. An aura of success replaced the previously pervasive doubt. Oliver, who had been deemed incapable of leading a "normal" life, had defied expectations.

Following this unexpected excursion, the doctor and I engaged in a conversation that resonated with hope and emotion. The doctor started out by saying, "I must admit, I didn't expect this amount of progress. Oliver's progress under your guidance is incredible."

"It's a testament to the resilience of these incredible children and the power of understanding," I said, tears welling up in my eyes. Oliver has shown us that autism is a journey rather than a diagnosis.

With a look of renewed respect, the doctor nodded. "He can now live like other kids, explore his potential, and contribute to the world in meaningful ways," they said.

Gratitude wells up in my heart as I think back on this unexpected journey. Despite its difficulties, our journey through the spectrum has served as a monument to the human spirit's resiliency and the transformational potential of understanding.

Not only is this book, **"The Art of Parenting an Autistic Child,"** a story of our journey, but it also serves as a roadmap and a friend for families traveling along similar roads. Its pages include the tactics that changed Oliver's course—a road map created with compassion, wisdom, and a steadfast confidence in every child's potential.

May our story be a ray of hope that shines through the difficulties for families navigating the same spectrum. Because there is a symphony of possibilities waiting to be found, acknowledged, and welcomed inside the spectrum.

Chapter one

Understanding Autism Spectrum Disorder (ASD)

Within the complex tapestry of human experience, cultural perspectives have a kaleidoscopic effect on how autism spectrum disorder (ASD) is seen. These viewpoints have occasionally been clouded by misinterpretation, which has led to the perpetuation of stereotypes that fall short of accurately expressing the essence of people who are autistic. We must start our journey by accepting that the prism through which society views autism has changed throughout time, but that changes are still necessary. Let's explore the core of this chapter, aiming to expand on our comprehension and accept the range of individuality that characterizes autism.

The Meaning of Autism Spectrum Disorder?

A neurodevelopmental disorder known as autism spectrum disorder causes a variety of difficulties with behavior and social communication. The word "spectrum" itself emphasizes how diverse this illness is, recognizing that people with ASD might have a broad range of strengths, skills, and areas of difficulty. Autism Spectrum Disorder (ASD) is a chronic illness that affects how people see and interact with the world. It is frequently diagnosed in early infancy.

Characteristics of Autism

Fundamentally, a distinct set of characteristics that influence the lives of individuals on the spectrum constitute autism. Even while every person is unique, some shared characteristics offer a foundation for comprehending the illness. Difficulties with both verbal and nonverbal expression are indicative of social communication challenges. Reciprocal communication, reading social signs, and grasping the subtleties of social interactions can be difficult for those with ASD.

Two other characteristics that are frequently seen in people with ASD are repetitive behaviors and a propensity for regularity. For people on the spectrum, these actions may provide a sense of security and comfort by providing an organized environment in an otherwise uncertain outside world. Autism sufferers' distinct experiences are further enhanced by abnormalities in their sensory processing, which affects how they perceive and react to environmental stimuli.

It is crucial to stress that, even though these traits offer a comprehensive picture of autism, the spectrum is dynamic and varied. The richness of this variation is found in the various ways people with autism traverse the world, each contributing their perspectives, abilities, and capabilities to the larger fabric of human existence. Our objective as we move deeper into this chapter is to promote a more complex and sympathetic understanding of autism, setting the groundwork for skillful and considerate parenting.

Core Features of ASD

A unique collection of fundamental characteristics that influence how people with autism spectrum disorder (ASD) see, engage with, and move through their environment are what define the disorder. These core ideas offer a basis for comprehending the difficulties and assets that come with autism. Having a thorough understanding of these fundamental characteristics is essential for parents raising children with ASD to provide them with the necessary assistance and guidance.

1. Difficulties in Social Communication

Social communication is one of the characteristics that set Autism Spectrum Disorder apart. People who are on the autism spectrum may have trouble understanding social cues, having productive conversations with others, and understanding the subtleties of interpersonal relationships. In-depth techniques for improving social communication abilities, developing deep relationships, and setting up settings that encourage social engagement for kids with autism will be covered in this chapter.

2. Habitual Activities and Opposition to Change

ASD is widely characterized by repetitive activities and a strong fondness for regularity. For people on the spectrum, these actions can offer stability in an otherwise chaotic environment by offering a sense of security and predictability. Parents who want to create supportive home environments must comprehend the significance of regularity and the function that repetitive behaviors play. We'll examine some useful tips for controlling and utilizing these traits in this chapter.

3. Variations in Sensory Processing

Many people with ASD have abnormalities in their sensory processing, which can cause them to be either overly or underly sensitive to different kinds of stimuli like sounds, lights, or textures. This particular component of autism has a big impact on how a kid feels about and engages with their surroundings. To safeguard their child's comfort and well-being, parents can discover information in this book on how to create sensory-friendly locations, implement sensory diets, and manage sensory problems.

As we examine these fundamental characteristics, we hope to shed light on the difficulties faced by people with ASD while also highlighting their distinct abilities and viewpoints. Parents may create a nurturing environment that supports their child's individuality and paves the way for a rewarding and encouraging parenting journey by acknowledging and appreciating these fundamental characteristics.

Spectrum Variability

One of the most important aspects of the wide spectrum of autism spectrum disorder (ASD) that requires our attention is the astonishing variety that each person on the spectrum exhibits. Autism is a broad spectrum of abilities, problems, and characteristics rather than a one-size-fits-all illness. Understanding the distinct requirements and assets of every child on the spectrum requires an appreciation of this variety.

The significance of customized approaches is highlighted by spectrum heterogeneity within the framework of this book on raising children with autism. Parenting techniques must be flexible and adaptive because what works well for one child might not be as beneficial for another. This chapter will discuss how to work within this range, adjusting strategies for support, communication, and treatments to meet the unique requirements of each kid. Understanding spectrum variety becomes a compass for parents as they set out on this journey, pointing them in the direction of a strategy that respects their child's individuality.

Common Co-occurring Conditions

Rarely does autism occur in isolation, and co-occurring illnesses, often known as comorbidities, are frequently experienced by people on the spectrum. These extra illnesses can include anything from physical and mental health problems to difficulties with cognition and development. According to this book, giving children with autism comprehensive and all-encompassing support requires an awareness of and response to common co-occurring illnesses.

Parents must comprehend the interactions that exist between autism and these related disorders. The co-occurrence of diseases such as attention-deficit/hyperactivity disorder (ADHD), anxiety disorders, or intellectual disabilities can have a substantial effect on a child's everyday functioning and developmental trajectory. We will explore methods in this chapter for recognizing, handling, and looking for suitable solutions for these extra problems. By doing this, parents may guarantee a more inclusive and customized approach to parenting while navigating the difficulties of their child's distinct personality.

Our goal as we examine spectrum variability and common co-occurring conditions is to provide parents with the information and resources they need to accept the variety that exists within the autistic spectrum. With this knowledge, parents may create a setting that highlights their kids' accomplishments while addressing their difficulties, encouraging a comprehensive and individualized approach to raising autistic kids.

Early Signs and Diagnosis

Parenting children with autism spectrum disorder (ASD) frequently starts with early detection of symptoms, which is a crucial step towards receiving a diagnosis. This part will examine the crucial elements of early indicators and the diagnostic procedure, stressing the significance of prompt detection and action. Recognizing the subtleties of these early routes is critical for caregivers, educators, and parents.

Identifying Early Red Flags

Acknowledging the early warning signs of Autism Spectrum Disorder (ASD) is an essential part of the parenting process. Even though each child is different and grows at their rate, some indicators call for more careful observation and possibly even intervention. Several typical early warning signs include:

1. **Social Difficulties**
   - Making little to no eye contact with others.
   - Disinterest in or insensitivity to social cues, including gestures and smiles.
   - Difficulty exchanging information back and forth, such as paying attention to someone else or answering their name.

2. **Communication Challenges**
   - Absence or delayed development of speech.
   - The use of gestures, such as pointing and waving, is restricted.
   - Inability to read and interpret nonverbal cues, such as body language or facial expressions.

3. **Repeated Actions**
   - Doing repetitive tasks or motions, such as rocking or flapping one's hands.
   - Resistance to routine adjustments or insistence on consistency.

4. **Sensory Sensitivities**
   - Either being overly or underly sensitive to sounds, textures, or other sensory inputs.

- Unusual fondness for or dislike of particular tastes, scents, or sensations.

It is advised that parents and other adults keep a close eye on their child's behavior and development and compare developmental milestones to normal course. Frequent developmental check-ups and consultations with medical specialists can assist in identifying any potential problem areas and help parents choose the right tests and treatments.

The Importance of Early Intervention

For kids with ASD, early intervention is essential to optimizing their developmental outcomes. Early infancy is a crucial time for neural plasticity and brain development, which makes prompt intervention extremely effective. This is the main reason that early intervention is crucial:

1. The plasticity of the brain

Early childhood interventions can make use of neuroplasticity, which allows the brain to be highly adaptive, to enhance the development of critical abilities.

2. Acquiring Skills

Key developmental domains like behavior, social skills, and communication are the focus of early intervention, which improves a child's capacity to learn and use these abilities.

3. Family Engagement

Early intervention programs frequently engage the family and provide parents with tools to enhance the development of their kids. A supportive environment is created at home by using a family-centered strategy.

4. Better Long-Term Results

Early intervention programs are associated with better long-term results for children, including increased social communication, academic success, and independence, according to research that is continuously conducted on the subject.

Early identification and resolution of developmental issues enables parents to work in conjunction with experts to customize interventions to meet the unique requirements of their child, laying the groundwork for future success.

Evaluations and the Diagnostic Process

Comprehensive testing is usually done for autism spectrum disorder by a multidisciplinary team of medical specialists. The following are the steps in the diagnostic process:

1. Screening for development

To detect possible developmental delays or issues, pediatricians may do developmental screenings at well-child visits.

2. Entire Assessment

If screening produces concerns, a thorough assessment is carried out. A group of experts, including occupational therapists, psychologists, and speech-language pathologists, evaluate several facets of the child's growth in this process.

3. Diagnostic Standards

The Diagnostic and Statistical Manual of Mental Disorders (DSM-5) provides standardized diagnostic criteria that form the basis of the evaluation. Restrictions and repeated habits are among the criteria, as are deficits in social communication.

4. Parental Contribution

To properly diagnose their child, parents must share details about their child's developmental history, behaviors, and any worries they may have.

5. Working together

Professional collaboration is common in the diagnostic procedure, which guarantees a thorough awareness of the child's strengths and challenges.

6. Continuous Observation

The diagnostic process is a continuous procedure that entails regular monitoring and reevaluation to modify therapies in response to a child's changing requirements.

Parents who are aware of the diagnostic process are better able to advocate for their child's needs and actively participate in their child's examination. It also makes it easier to collaborate with medical specialists to develop a personalized and successful support plan that is suited to each child's particular needs.

Positive Framing and Neurodiversity

The ideas of neurodiversity and positive framing surface in the discourse surrounding autism spectrum disorder (ASD) as transforming lenses through which to perceive and comprehend the varied experiences of people on the spectrum. This part delves into the fundamentals of neurodiversity, the significance of redefining autism, and the advantages of creating a supportive atmosphere.

Acknowledging Neurodiversity

This concept acknowledges and values the inherent differences in brain activity between people. It contends that variations in neurocognitive functioning are an essential component of the human experience, challenging the conventional understanding of neurological differences as aberrations from the norm. Accepting neurological variances as desirable and necessary components of the complexity of human cognition, particularly those linked to autism, is a key component of embracing neurodiversity.

When it comes to autism, embracing neurodiversity means realizing that people on the spectrum have special talents, viewpoints, and modes of interaction with the outside world. It is an appeal to stop pathologizingautism and to embrace the variety of ways that people with ASD interact with their environment. Accepting neurodiversity promotes a narrative that celebrates and acknowledges the intrinsic worth of neurocognitive diversity rather than one that is deficit-focused.

Changing Views Regarding Autism

Adopting a strength-based approach instead of deficit-based approaches is a necessary step in changing perceptions of autism. It entails redefining obstacles related to autism as chances for development, education, and original contributions. From this angle, the skills, abilities, and areas of competence of people with autism are highlighted rather than just the things they might struggle with. Changing one's viewpoint on autism is a powerful journey that entails appreciating and fostering the innate qualities of those who fall on the spectrum.

People with ASD are given the ability to take advantage of their special skills and abilities when they embrace a strengths-based approach. This way of thinking also embraces families and caregivers, enabling them to see their jobs as chances to accentuate and promote the positive traits in their loved ones. Changing attitudes toward autism promotes a society that values variety, resiliency, and the potential for ongoing development.

Fostering a Positive Environment

Recognizing and meeting the needs of a varied range of people is essential to fostering a healthy environment for those with autism. This includes inclusive practices that foster a sense of belonging, communication aids, and sensory-friendly surroundings. Additionally, accessibility, comprehension, and tolerance for neurodiversity are given top priority in positive situations.

A positive atmosphere is one in which people with autism are celebrated for who they are, as well as accepted. Promoting inclusive behaviors in the workplace, in the community, and education is part of this. It takes proactive measures to dismantle obstacles, confront prejudices, and establish an inclusive culture that goes beyond awareness to true comprehension and inclusivity to cultivate a pleasant atmosphere.

The ideas of neurodiversity and positive framing, taken together, represent a paradigm shift that, rather than pathologizing differences, celebrates the special abilities and viewpoints that people with autism provide to society. A society that honors and uplifts every person, regardless of their neurocognitive profile, can be created by embracing neurodiversity, changing perceptions, and establishing positive settings.

EXERCISES

Reflecting on Preconceptions:

- What were your initial thoughts and feelings when you first learned about your child's autism diagnosis?
- How has your understanding of autism evolved since that initial moment?
- In what ways has this evolving understanding positively influenced your interactions with your child?

Further Education Goal:

- Set a goal for further educating yourself about autism to deepen your understanding of autism.
- Describe how you intend to incorporate this newfound knowledge into your parenting approach.

Chapter two

Creating a Supportive Home Environment

The key to raising children with autism spectrum disorder (ASD) effectively is to have a loving and supportive home environment. As we explore the details of this chapter, our attention moves to the household, which serves as the very starting point of a child's developmental journey. The key components of creating a nurturing environment for kids on the autism spectrum are examined in this chapter. In addition to meeting their child's specific needs, parents will learn how to create an environment that supports growth, comfort, and a sense of security. This includes everything from creating sensory-friendly spaces to implementing effective communication strategies.

Establishing a Systematic Process

Creating a schedule that is structured is essential to creating a stable and supportive home environment for children with autism spectrum disorder (ASD). The significance of predictability, the creation of visual schedules, and the implementation of daily routines are examined in this part as crucial elements in building an organized framework for kids on the autism spectrum.

The Value of Predictability

Foundational Stability: An organized routine is based on predictability, which acts as its cornerstone. Predictability gives children with ASD a sense of security and comfort since they frequently flourish in surroundings that are defined by regularity and familiarity. Emotional control is supported and anxiety is decreased when one knows what to anticipate in different scenarios. Children can navigate their daily lives with more confidence and control because of this consistency.

Reducing Stress and Anxiety: People with autism may find it especially difficult to deal with the unpredictable nature of unexpected situations. Parents can reduce worry and stress by establishing predictability in their daily routines. In addition to helping the child, this stress reduction also makes the family dynamic more harmonious and well-balanced.

Creating Visual Schedules

Visual Aids for Clarity: For kids with ASD, visual schedules are an effective way to establish a disciplined daily routine. These visual aids offer a concrete and understandable means of conveying the order of events or activities. Visual schedules, whether in the form of words, symbols, or pictures, provide youngsters with clarity and a better understanding of what is expected of them each day. To help with seamless transitions between duties, a visual schedule can, for example, incorporate pictures of morning routines, school activities, and evening customs.

Tailored and Adaptable: One of the benefits of visual schedules is that they may be tailored to meet specific needs and preferences. They can be customized to fit each child's individual needs, taking into account things like their communication preferences, comprehension level, and sensory issues. Parents can improve their children's engagement and foster a sense of control over their routine by allowing them to participate in the creation of their visual timetable.

Creating Daily Routines

Regularities offer a structure for consistency, which strengthens the predictability that is crucial for kids with ASD. Meals, playtimes, and bedtime customs are just a few examples of the different facets of the day that can be included in these routines. Daily routine consistency helps children acquire critical life skills and self-control in addition to supporting their awareness of the world around them.

A major issue for many autistic people is making the transitions between activities seamless with well-established daily routines. Parents can help their kids transition more smoothly by using visual signals and being consistent. This can help kids feel less stressed and more secure while switching between tasks.

Essentially, establishing a routine is incorporating daily consistency, visual aids, and predictability into every aspect of everyday living. A visual timetable that outlines the procedures for getting ready for school, having breakfast, and dressing in the morning is one example of this. By making these deliberate efforts, parents may create a nurturing home that not only meets the special needs of their kid with ASD but also establishes the foundation for a happy and secure family life.

Sensory-Friendly Spaces

Within the realm of raising children diagnosed with Autism Spectrum Disorder (ASD), the idea of sensory-friendly environments assumes a central role as a crucial component of setting up a home that accommodates the distinct sensory processing difficulties experienced by those on the spectrum. To improve the general well-being of children with ASD, this part investigates the art of creating sensory-friendly places and dives into the knowledge of issues related to sensory processing.

Recognizing the Difficulties of Sensory Processing

Autism and Sensory Processing: People with ASD frequently have abnormalities in their sensory processing, which affects how they take in and react to environmental events. Hypersensitivity (over-reactivity) or hyposensitivity (under-responsiveness) to stimuli like sounds, lights, textures, and odors might be signs of these sensory processing issues. Comprehending these discrepancies is essential to customizing residential settings that suit and enhance the sensory requirements of kids on the autism spectrum.

Effect on Daily Life: Problems with sensory processing can have a big influence on daily routines and activities. For instance, a youngster who is hypersensitive to some sounds would find being in busy places upsetting, whereas a hypersensitive child to touch might seek out intense pressure feelings. Acknowledging and resolving these issues helps to establish a sensory-friendly home environment that encourages the kid to feel secure, peaceful, and safe.

Modifying Living Areas to Promote Sensory Comfort

As a transformative approach to designing surroundings that cater to the specific sensory demands of people on the spectrum, the idea of modifying home spaces for sensory comfort becomes apparent in the process of parenting children with autism spectrum disorder (ASD). This section looks into ways to create sensory-friendly environments in the home and examines how to use them as powerful tools for enhancing sensory well-being.

How to Create Sensory-Friendly Environments

Making Havens of Comfort: Specifically planned locations in the house that address the special sensory requirements of kids with ASD are known as sensory-friendly spaces. These areas are designed to be safe havens where kids can manage their experiences and get controlled sensory stimulation. Spaces that are friendly to the senses may take lighting, sound, textures, and organization into account.

Adaptable Environments: Areas designed with children's sensory needs in mind can be made to suit each child's unique preferences. A bedroom that is sensory-friendly could, for instance, have soft lighting, noise-canceling technology, and tactile components like soft textures or weighted blankets. These rooms are flexible enough to change to accommodate a child's evolving sensory needs.

Including Sensory Instruments: Equipment and instruments intended to give particular kinds of sensory input are frequently seen in sensory-friendly locations. Fidget toys, sensory swings, and soothing sensory bins are a few examples. These carefully selected tools can assist children in self-regulating and managing sensory input, taking into account their unique sensory profile.

Recognizing the specific sensory demands of children with ASD, comprehending sensory processing difficulties, and designing sensory-friendly environments are, at their core, artistic endeavors. In a world that can occasionally feel overwhelming, parents can create a haven where their children can grow, explore, and find comfort by designing their home environments to encourage sensory well-being.

Strategies for a Sensory Diet

The phrase "sensory diet" describes a customized regimen of exercises and methods created to address each person's unique sensory requirements. Including sensory diet techniques in everyday routines can help children with ASD achieve comfort and regulation of their senses. Comprehending and putting these tactics into practice aids in the general modification of living environments for improved sensory well-being.

Determining Sensory Preferences:

A thorough grasp of a person's sensory profile is the first step in developing a sensory diet. Parents can learn about their child's specific sensory preferences, sensitivities, and calming techniques through observation and conversation. The cornerstone for customizing the home environment to satisfy particular sensory needs is this individual insight.

1. **Sensory Activities:** Proprioceptive, vestibular, tactile, auditory, and visual inputs are only a few of the various sensory modalities that are targeted by sensory diet tactics. Activities for a sensory diet could be:

2. **Deep Pressure Exercises:** Apply compression clothing, weighted blankets, or light massage.

3. **Vestibular Activities:** Taking part in coordinated motions, such as swinging or rocking.

4. **Tactile Activities:** Using textured surfaces, tactile items, or sensory bins, explore textures.

5. **Visual and aural Activities:** Using calming lighting or relaxing music, you can create a peaceful visual and aural atmosphere.

Including Sensory Tools:

Using sensory tools is essential for putting sensory diet plans into practice in home environments. These devices can be thoughtfully incorporated into everyday routines and are intended to offer particular sensory input. Among the sensory tools are, for instance:

- **Fidget toys:** provide tactile stimulation to aid in controlling oneself.
- **Chewable Items:** Providing comfort and focus through oral sensory input.
- **Sensory swings or seating:**Opportunities for vestibular input are provided through this approach.

Creating Consistency:

When putting sensory diet ideas into practice, consistency is essential. Parents can give their children a consistent and comforting sensory experience by including tools and activities in everyday routines. Regular exposure to sensory inputs enhances general well-being and self-regulation.

In conclusion, modifying living environments for sensory comfort entails carefully incorporating sensory diet plans customized to meet the specific requirements of kids with ASD. Parents may build surroundings that honor their child's unique sensory experiences and promote comfort, regulation, and general sensory well-being by learning about their child's preferences, implementing sensory activities, and using sensory tools.

Effective Communication Techniques

These techniques serve as cornerstones of connection when it comes to raising children with autism spectrum disorder (ASD), providing a conduit for comprehension and expression. This part explores the subtleties of improving communication abilities, the incorporation of visual aids and supports, and the intricate process of social communication development. By thoroughly examining these aspects, parents can foster a communication atmosphere that supports the distinct abilities and difficulties of their autistic kid.

Improving Interpersonal Communication Capabilities

Customized Communication Strategies:

Improving communication abilities necessitates acknowledging the uniqueness of every child's communication preferences. A tailored approach is crucial for kids with ASD, who could struggle with both verbal and nonverbal communication. Parents can encourage dialogue through:

- Promoting the use of preferred communication methods, such as augmentative and alternative communication (AAC) systems, sign language, or verbal language.
- Identifying and reacting to nonverbal clues, including body language, gestures, and facial expressions.
- Establishing an atmosphere that values communication and inspires the youngster to start and participate in conversations.

Encouraging Functional Communication:

The goal of functional communication is to give children useful tools to communicate their wants, needs, and emotions. This includes:

- Introducing and practicing communication skills that apply to a child's day-to-day experiences.
- Using images, symbols, or visual aids to help communicate ideas.
- Including the child's preferences and areas of interest in communication activities will increase involvement.

Communication Tools and Visual Supports

Visual aids as Communication Tools:

These aids are essential for helping people with ASD communicate. These resources offer visual aids that help improve communication and understanding. Among the strategies are:

- Creating attractive plans that show off everyday activities and routines.
- Use symbols or visual cues to convey ideas, options, or job phases.
- Social stories are used to clarify social circumstances and appropriate conduct.

Augmentative and alternative communication (AAC):

Since verbal communication can be difficult for certain people with ASD, AAC systems are helpful resources. AAC uses techniques like:

- Systems known as picture communication systems (PECS) employ pictures to convey ideas and language.
- Devices that produce speech and allow people to speak.
- Tools for written communication for people who gain from writing.

Fostering Social Communication

Building Social Communication Skills:

Cultivating social communication skills includes building the capacity for mutually beneficial social interactions. Among the strategies are:

- Focusing the child's attention on shared items or activities to promote collaborative attention.
- Turn-taking in play and conversation should be taught and practiced.
- Establishing planned social events to promote social interaction.

Stressing Non-Verbal Communication:

An essential part of social contact is non-verbal communication. Parents can encourage their child to develop nonverbal communication skills by:

- Promoting the use of body language, gestures, and pointing.
- Demonstrating suitable nonverbal clues using your face and eye contact.
- Adding visual aids to improve comprehension of social cues.

To put it simply, functional communication, using visual supports, accepting individuality, and encouraging the development of social communication skills are all important components of effective communication techniques for children with ASD. Parents can foster a communicative environment that enhances their child's capacity for connection, expression, and engagement with the world around them by customizing their approaches to each child's distinct strengths and problems.

EXERCISES

Creating a Supportive Space:

- List potential sensory triggers in your home environment.
- What changes have you implemented to make your home more sensory-friendly?
- What is your child's reaction to these modifications? Document any positive observations in behavior, increased comfort or expression of joy.

Community Engagement:

- Share your experiences and the changes you've made with a supportive community to exchange ideas .
- What insights or suggestions did you gain from this community engagement?

Chapter three

Navigating Educational Systems

This chapter takes readers on a tour through the complex educational systems that come with raising children with autism spectrum disorder (ASD). The complexity of Individualized Education Programs (IEPs), a vital component of providing customized educational support for kids on the autism spectrum, is explained in this chapter. This chapter delves into the skill of working with school teams, defending the right to necessary services, and keeping an eye on the status of IEPs to create a learning environment that values diversity and encourages the complete development of every child.

Individualized EducationPrograms (IEPs)

IEPs are specialized learning plans created to address the particular requirements of students with disabilities, including ASD students. IEPs are detailed plans that support a child's academic and developmental success by providing services, adjustments, and educational goals.

Working Together with School Teams

Education partnership:

Collaborating with school teams is a cooperative approach that calls for open communication and group decision-making. Important elements of this partnership consist of:

1. **Team Dynamics:** Putting together a cohesive and open-minded group of parents, educators, special education specialists, and other pertinent experts.
2. **Information sharing:** Giving detailed details on the child's preferences, strengths, and difficulties so that the IEP may be developed with that knowledge in mind.
3. **Active Participation:** Bringing new perspectives to IEP meetings, speaking out for the needs of the kid, and actively engaging in them.

Developing a Unified Vision:

The foundation of successful cooperation with school teams is the development of a cohesive educational vision for the child. This includes:

- Deciding on shared objectives that complement the child's unique needs and ambitions.
- Creating plans and plans of action that address issues and build on the child's strengths.
- Promoting constant contact and input to modify the IEP as the child develops.

Advocating for the Right Services

Promoting Educational Rights:

Ensuring that the IEP corresponds with the child's educational needs requires vigorous advocacy for appropriate services. This includes:

1. **Recognizing Legal Rights:** To effectively advocate for a child's rights, one must become familiar with the federal and state laws about special education.
2. **Clarifying Services:** Outlining in detail the precise services, concessions, and adjustments required to promote the learning and growth of the kid.
3. **Collaboration and negotiation:** Having a positive conversation with school staff to identify solutions that work for both parties and make sure the child's needs are addressed.

Stressing Inclusivity:

Promoting inclusivity in the educational setting requires advocacy that goes beyond personal needs. This comprises:

- Promoting inclusive methods that allow the child to attend general education classes.
- Encouraging an inclusive and encouraging environment in the school community by raising awareness and understanding of autism.

Monitoring IEP progress

Continuous Evaluation and Adjustment:

Monitoring IEP progress is an ongoing process that involves continuous assessment and adjustment. Key considerations include:

1. **Data collection:** Gathering information regularly to evaluate the child's advancement toward the goals and objectives of the IEP.
2. **Progress Meetings:**Attending these meetings with school teams to go over statistics, talk about successes, and work through any new issues that may come up.
3. **Modifications and Revisions:** Working together to make necessary adjustments and revisions to the IEP so that it continues to be responsive to the child's changing needs.

Developing Parents' Advocacy Skills:

Giving parents the tools they need to effectively advocate for their children's education entails:

- Supplying parents with information and instruction to improve their comprehension of the IEP procedure and their place within it.
- Building self-assurance and self-advocacy in parents to enable them to effectively communicate their child's needs.

This section has essentially negotiated the complexity of educational systems, emphasizing IEPs as unique road maps for academic achievement. Parents play a critical role in creating an educational environment that recognizes the special abilities and potential of children with ASD by encouraging cooperation, fighting for necessary assistance, and keeping an eye on their children's development.

Strategies for Inclusive Education

This section delves deeper into the area of inclusive education strategies within the larger context of raising children with autism spectrum disorder (ASD). This chapter focuses on creating inclusive and diverse learning settings, delving into the nuances of inclusive classrooms, fostering peer connections, and assisting children with autism spectrum disorders in participating in social situations.

The cornerstone of creating varied and encouraging learning environments is inclusive education practices. These tactics are intended to guarantee that kids with ASD have fair access to education, participate fully in the educational process, and flourish in inclusive learning environments.

Encouraging Classroom Inclusivity

Developing an Inclusive Culture:

Encouraging inclusive classrooms requires creating a culture that celebrates variety and recognizes the individual characteristics of every student. Important elements consist of:

1. **Teacher Training:** Offering educators ongoing professional development to improve their knowledge of autism and inclusive teaching methods.
2. **Differentiated instructions:** This refers to modifying teaching strategies to meet the needs of students with a range of learning styles, including those linked to ASD.
3. **Universal Design for Learning (UDL):**Using the concepts of UDL, learning environments can be made adaptable and accessible for all students.

Accommodations and Modifications:

The following are put into place to guarantee that students with ASD are included:

1. **Individualized Supports:** Providing specially designed accommodations for each child's individual needs as specified in their IEP.
2. **Assistive technology:**Using technological tools and resources to enhance communication and learning.
3. **Collaborative Planning:** Coordinating educational practices with individual goals through collaborative planning sessions with parents, teachers, and support workers.

Establishing Peer Connections

Peer Interaction and Collaboration:

Promoting constructive interactions and teamwork between kids with ASD and their peers is a key component of building peer relationships. Among the strategies are:

1. **Peer Support Programs:** Putting in place organized programs for peers to help and hang out with neurotypical peers.
2. **Social Skills Training**: Including instruction in social skills to improve students' interpersonal abilities in the curriculum.
3. **Buddy Systems:** Creating buddy networks to connect students with ASD to neurotypical classmates to provide friendship and support.

Education on Autism Awareness:

Creating a culture of tolerance and empathy among students is facilitated by increasing awareness of autism:

1. **Classroom Presentations:**Age-appropriate lectures regarding autism should be facilitated in classrooms to raise awareness and debunk myths.
2. **Inclusive Activities:**Incorporating inclusive activities that foster cooperation, unity, and understanding between people.

Encouragement of Social Inclusion

Holistic Social Development:

Promoting social inclusion includes tactics that support kids with ASD in their overall social development. Important things to think about are:

- Providing organized social opportunities, like group projects or cooperative activities, is a way to foster social contact.
- Encouraging neurotypical peers to exhibit inclusive behavior and constructive social interactions is known as peer modeling.

- Encouraging involvement in extracurricular activities to increase social horizons is known as extracurricular involvement.

Building a Supportive Environment:

Encouraging adolescents with ASD to participate in social activities requires the establishment of a supportive environment.

1. **Anti-Bullying Initiatives:** Putting anti-bullying initiatives into place to guarantee a supportive and safe school environment, more details on this is discussed in the coming sub-chapter.
2. **Customized Support Plans:** Creating customized support plans that cater to every student's particular social needs.

Essentially, inclusive education strategies serve as the cornerstone of an educational strategy that promotes the social inclusion of children with ASD, builds meaningful peer relationships, and celebrates variety. Together, educators and parents create an educational environment that recognizes and supports each learner's strengths and needs by encouraging inclusive classrooms, fostering peer relationships, and encouraging social inclusion.

Addressing Bullying and Social Challenges

This phase explores the important issue of Addressing Bullying and Social Challenges within the complicated terrain of parenting children with Autism Spectrum Disorder (ASD). This chapter outlines methods for identifying bullying indicators, imparts critical social skills, and places a strong emphasis on building a peer support system to promote the emotional health and social inclusion of kids on the autistic spectrum.

Resolving bullying and social issues requires providing teachers, peers, and students with ASD with the resources they need to establish inclusive, respectful, and safe social environments in classrooms.

Recognizing Signs of Bullying

Vigilance and Awareness:

In order to spot the early warning signs of bullying, parents, educators and peers need to be more watchful and aware of their surroundings. Important components consist of:

1. **Behavioral Changes:**Abrupt shifts in behavior, attitude, or emotional state that could point to discomfort are referred to as behavioral alterations.
2. **Social Withdrawal:**Identifying indicators of social disengagement, such as unwillingness to go to school or avoidance of particular locations.
3. **Inexplicable physical or Emotional Changes:** Keep an eye out for evidence of emotional turmoil, damaged belongings, or inexplicable injuries.

Open Communication:

Recognizing bullying symptoms also requires building a trustworthy environment and keeping lines of communication open with the youngster.

1. **Promoting Disclosure:** Establishing a safe environment where kids feel at ease talking about their experiences.
2. **Frequent Check-ins:** Talking about social contacts and addressing any issues or problems during regular check-ins.

Teaching Social Skills

Providing social skills education is essential to enabling kids with ASD to successfully negotiate social situations. Among the strategies are

1. **Explicit Instructions:**Giving clear instructions on social cues, expectations, and conventions is known as explicit instruction.
2. **Role-playing:** Practicing and reinforcing suitable social responses through role-playing scenarios.
3. **Social Stories:** Using this approach to guide appropriate behavior and explain social circumstances.

Peer-Mediated Interventions:

Using neurotypical peers' support to further build social skills

- Encouraging neurotypical peers to exhibit inclusive and supportive behavior is known as peer modeling.
- Peer buddy programs can be established to promote understanding and constructive social connections.

Establishing a Helpful Peer Environment

Cultivating Inclusive Friendships:

Establishing inclusive friendships that advance understanding and empathy is essential to building a supportive peer environment.

- Creating inclusive activities that promote cooperation, shared interests, and teamwork.
- Putting into practice classroom initiatives that prioritize acceptance, kindness, and empathy.
- Encouraging a culture that values and embraces neurodiversity is part of celebrating differences.

Anti-Bullying Programs:

Putting anti-bullying initiatives into formalized frameworks helps foster a polite and secure learning environment.

1. **Educational Campaigns:** Putting into practice initiatives that increase public knowledge of bullying, its effects, and prevention methods.
2. **Responsive Protocol:**Establishing explicit procedures for handling and quickly responding to instances of bullying is known as "responsive protocols."

Addressing Bullying and Social Challenges essentially entails taking proactive steps to identify warning indicators of bullying, impart critical social skills, and foster a positive peer environment. To create safe and respectful social settings where children with ASD can thrive emotionally and socially, parents, educators, and peers work together to promote open communication, provide explicit teaching in social skills, and build inclusive connections.

EXERCISES

Understanding Your Child's Educational Needs:

> - Review your child's Individualized Education Program (IEP) or educational plan.
> - Identify one aspect of the plan that has been particularly effective. What improvements have you observed?

Challenges and Strategies:

> - Identify challenges your child has faced in the educational setting.
> - List potential strategies or accommodations to address these challenges.

Educator Collaboration:

> - Schedule a meeting with your child's educators to discuss your observations and potential adjustments to the educational plan.
> - Document any positive outcomes or insights gained from these discussions.

Chapter four

Therapeutic Interventions

This chapter explores approaches that promote the well-being and developmental growth of children with autism spectrum disorder (ASD) by delving into the field of therapeutic interventions. In this chapter, we look at the basic ideas behind Applied Behavior Analysis (ABA), how it may be used at home, and how important it is to view development through the prism of ABA.

Applied Behavior Analysis (ABA)

The goal of Applied Behavior Analysis (ABA), a method based on science and evidence, is to comprehend and change behavior. ABA was first created as a therapeutic intervention for people with autism, but it has now expanded to be widely utilized to treat a wide range of behavioral issues in a variety of demographics. The fundamentals of ABA consist of a collection of ideas and methods meant to increase desired behaviors and decrease undesirable ones.

The fundamentals of ABA

Recognizing the fundamental ideas and techniques of ABA is necessary to comprehend its foundations:

1. Behavioral evaluation:

The first step in ABA is a comprehensive behavioral evaluation, which entails methodically obtaining data to comprehend the purpose and patterns of behavior. Important elements consist of:

Target Behavior Identification: Identifying the actions that will be the subject of the intervention. These could be certain behaviors like social interactions, communication abilities, or unhelpful habits that need to change.

Antecedents and Consequences: Analyzing the circumstances or occurrences (antecedents) that lead up to the target behavior and the outcomes that ensue is known as "antecedents and consequences." This aids in locating trends and catalysts.

2. Behavioral treatments:

After identifying the target behaviors, ABA creates treatments that are grounded in behavioral principles to effect positive change. Among the fundamental components of behavioral treatments are:

Positive Reinforcement: Using positive rewards to make desired behaviors more likely to occur is known as positive reinforcement. To reinforce a behavior, this entails offering prizes or incentives right away.

Negative Reinforcement: Removing or avoiding unpleasant stimuli to make a behavior more likely to occur is known as negative reinforcement. In contrast to punishment, this entails setting up circumstances that allow the person to flee or avoid discomfort.

Punishment: Imposing penalties to make undesirable actions less likely. When feasible, ABA promotes the use of positive reinforcement rather than punishment.

3. Data collecting:

A key component of ABA is data collecting, which emphasizes methodical and objective observation. This includes:

Measurement: Putting behaviors into observable, quantifiable terms so that precise data can be gathered.

Baseline Data: Gathering information before implementing treatments to determine the frequency, duration, and severity of target behaviors as they already exist.

Ongoing Monitoring: Gathering information both during and after actions to evaluate results and make informed decisions.

4. Customized Plans:

ABA acknowledges the individuality of every person and designs interventions to fulfill their particular requirements. This includes:

Setting Clear Goals: Specifying quantifiable objectives that take into account the person's strengths, weaknesses, and developmental priorities.

Prompting and Shaping: Using cues or help, prompting and shaping work together to gradually lead an individual toward desirable actions by reinforcing successive approximations.

5. Generalization:

This is important to ABA because it makes sure that taught behaviors are transferable outside of the particular environments in which interventions are implemented. Among the generalization techniques are:

Changing Settings: Putting interventions into practice in diverse settings to encourage the transfer of abilities to new situations.

Various Stimuli: Promoting the use of taught behaviors in reaction to various stimuli, persons, and circumstances.

6. Positive Behavior Support:

The theory behind ABA is positive behavior support, which places more emphasis on actively promoting positive behaviors than it does on merely minimizing negative ones. This strategy entails:

Functional behavior assessment (FBA): FBAs are used to determine the reason or function of a behavior, which informs the creation of successful interventions.

Collaborative Planning: To guarantee consistency and generalizability of interventions, include parents, caregivers, educators, and other pertinent parties in the planning process.

To summarize, the fundamentals of Applied Behavior Analysis entail a methodical approach to comprehending, evaluating, and altering behavior. Through the use of concepts like tailored planning, continuous data gathering, and positive reinforcement, ABA offers a methodical framework for encouraging constructive behavioral modifications and improving people's general well-being.

Putting ABA into Practice at Home

Collaborative Home-Based Strategies:

Parents, caregivers, and professionals must work together to implement ABA at home.

- **Parent Education:** Educating parents in ABA to improve their ability to put techniques into practice.

- **Consistency:** Using ABA techniques to reinforce learning consistently.

Including ABA in Daily Routines:

Integrating ABA in everyday routines increases its efficacy.

- **Routine analysis:** This involves the evaluation of daily activities to find areas that could benefit from focused interventions.
- **Behavioral Support Plans:** Developing and putting into action behavioral support plans to deal with particular difficulties encountered throughout daily tasks.

Assessing Advancement in ABA

Data-Driven Progress Monitoring:

Assessing the advancement of ABA is a data-driven procedure that necessitates continuous evaluation and modification.

- **Data analysis:** The systematic examination of gathered information to evaluate behavioral shifts.
- **Intervention Adjustment:** Making changes to interventions in response to problems and observed improvement.
- **Collaborative Review:** To guarantee a comprehensive picture of progress, collaborative reviews involving ABA experts, educators, and parents are conducted.

Celebrating Success and Modifying Objectives:

Motivation and reinforcement come from acknowledging and applauding accomplishments.

- Using positive reinforcement to recognize and promote desired behaviors is known as positive reinforcement.
- Changing objectives in light of reached milestones and changing developmental requirements.

This chapter on therapeutic interventions essentially clarifies the critical role that applied behavior analysis, or ABA plays in fostering the development of children with ASD. Parents and other caregivers can harness the power of this research-based method to help their children achieve meaningful and good results by learning the fundamentals of ABA, putting it into practice together at home, and routinely assessing their progress.

Speech and LanguageTherapy

To help children with Autism Spectrum Disorder (ASD) overcome communication difficulties, speech and language therapy is covered in detail in this part. To empower people with ASD, this chapter delves into the nuances of treating communication challenges, investigating speech therapy strategies, and developing functional communication.

The goal of speech and language therapy is to help people with ASD communicate more effectively by addressing their difficulties and improving their capacity for self-expression and social interaction.

Communication Challenges in Autism

People diagnosed with Autism Spectrum Disorder frequently have distinct communication patterns characterized by difficulties in social interaction, language acquisition, and practical abilities. Important difficulties consist of:

1. **Social Communication Deficits:** Inability to read and interpret nonverbal signs in social situations, such as gestures and facial expressions.

2. **Delays in Speech and Language Milestones:** Individual differences in language learning can lead to delays in speech and language development.

3. **Literal Interpretation:** Propensity to take words at face value, which makes it difficult to understand idioms or figurative language.

Example of a Real-Life Scenario: Let's say that a child with Autism Spectrum Disorder has trouble understanding sarcasm. When a classmate remarks, "Nice going, Einstein!" in jest during a conversation, the child can take this as an actual insult and miss the joke's intended comedy. The goal of speech therapy would be to assist the youngster in understanding social cues and metaphorical language.

Speech Therapy Techniques

Speech therapy uses a range of methods to treat particular ASD-related communication difficulties. Methods consist of:

1. **Visual Supports:** Improving understanding and expression through the use of visual aids including images, graphs, and social stories.

2. **Augmentative and Alternative Communication (AAC):**Introducing this approach and its technologies to support people with limited verbal ability. These systems can take the form of communication boards, devices, or apps.

3. **Activities for Improving Speech Clarity and Articulation:** For those with speech sound impairments, these activities help with speech clarity and articulation.

An example of a real-life scenario would be a youngster with ASD who has trouble with articulation, making it difficult for others to comprehend what they are saying. During speech therapy sessions, patients may practice certain sounds using games, exercises, and visual cues to improve their overall speech intelligibility and articulation.

Promoting Functional Communication

The goal of speech-language therapy is to help people with ASD communicate their needs, wants, and ideas in a way that is clear and concise. Among the strategies are:

- Teaching people alternate, socially acceptable methods to express their wants and desires is known as functional communication training or FCT.

- Including instruction to improve pragmatic language abilities, such as taking turns, keeping eye contact, and recognizing conversational cues.

- Encouraging chances for people with ASD to practice social communication in authentic settings.

Example of a Real-Life Situation: Take the example of an ASD adolescent who finds it difficult to start and carry on discussions. Role-playing scenarios, greeting drills, and talking about how to join in on discussions with peers are all possible in speech therapy. The teenager gains the ability to start and take part in significant social contacts throughout time.

Speech-language therapy is essentially a transformative intervention that helps people with ASD who struggle with communication. Speech therapy plays a crucial role in helping people on the autism spectrum reach their full communication potential by using specialized strategies and encouraging functional communication. This opens the door to more meaningful interactions and expressive possibilities.

Sensory and Occupational Therapy

In this section, we'll concentrate on occupational and sensory therapies, which are crucial parts of providing children with autism spectrum disorder (ASD) with comprehensive treatment. This chapter discusses the importance of fine and gross motor skill development, dives into sensory integration techniques, and highlights the role of occupational therapy.

Sensory and Occupational Therapy are part of a complete strategy that addresses the various needs of people with Autism Spectrum Disorder (ASD), promotes skill development, and improves their capacity to interact meaningfully with their surroundings.

Importance of Occupational Therapy

Occupational therapy is essential to improving people with ASD's independence and everyday functioning. Important elements consist of:

1. **Self-Care Skills:** Managing difficulties with daily living activities (ADLs) including eating, dressing, and grooming.
2. **Sensory Processing:** Assisting people in controlling their sensory input and making it easier for them to engage in everyday activities.
3. **Fostering independence:** Do this by incorporating tasks appropriate for an individual's age and developmental stage.

Techniques for Integrating Senses

Effective management and processing of sensory information is made possible for people with ASD through the use of sensory integration strategies. Among the strategies are:

1. **Sensory diets:** Adapting exercises and sensory stimuli to each person's requirements, taking into account hyper- and hyposensitivity.
2. **Environmental Modifications:** Establishing comfortable, sensory-friendly spaces that reduce sensory overload.
3. **Techniques for desensitization:** Exposing people gradually to stimuli to lessen sensitivity and aversion.

Development of Fine and Gross Motor Skills

Occupational therapy's core goals include the development of fine and gross motor skills, which address coordination and motor control issues. Among the strategies are:

1. **Fine motor tasks:** These include scribbling, cutting with scissors, and holding small items. They also help to improve coordination and precision.
2. **Gross motor exercises:** Include drills to improve balance, coordination, and spatial awareness in addition to bigger motions.
3. **Play-based Interventions:** Presenting therapeutic play activities that combine the development of motor skills with pleasurable activities.

Imagine a child with ASD who has trouble with fine motor skills in the real world. This would affect their ability to write clearly. Activities like finger painting, picking up tiny objects with tweezers, and practicing letter formation in a sensory-friendly setting are a few examples of what occupational therapy sessions may entail. These interventions help to enhance handwriting abilities and fine motor control over time.

In conclusion, occupational therapy and sensory therapy stand out as essential components of the multifaceted support system for people with ASD. By highlighting the significance of occupational therapy, integrating strategies for sensory integration, and focusing on the development of fine and gross motor skills, this therapeutic approach fosters a comprehensive development that goes beyond symptom management to support overall health and functional independence.

EXERCISES

Applying Strategies at Home:

> ➤ Choose one therapeutic intervention discussed in the chapter (e.g., ABA) and implement a basic aspect of it at home.
> ➤ Keep a daily log of your child's responses and any changes in behavior.

Reflection and Feedback:

> ➤ Reflect on your experience after a week. What aspects of the therapeutic intervention worked well, and what challenges did you encounter?
> ➤ Share your experiences with your child's therapist or support network. Seek feedback and suggestions for refining the intervention at home.

Chapter five

Social and Emotional Development

This chapter will explore Social and Emotional Development in the complex journey of raising children with Autism Spectrum Disorder (ASD). It highlights the significant influence that emotional intelligence has on the well-being and social interactions of people on the spectrum. Emphasizing the importance of promoting emotional well-being for autistic children, this chapter clarifies understanding emotions in autism, teaching emotional literacy, identifying and controlling emotions, and handling anxiety and meltdowns.

Understanding Emotions in Autism

It can be difficult and incredibly enlightening for children with autism to make their way through the complex emotional environment. To build resilience and encourage social and emotional development, it is essential to comprehend the subtleties of emotional experiences.

Fostering Emotional Intelligence

Teaching emotional literacy entails giving autistic kids the language and understanding skills they need to communicate and comprehend emotions. Among the strategies are:

1. **Visual Supports:** Labeling and illustrating various emotions with the use of visual aids like emotion charts or flashcards including facial expressions.
2. **Storytelling:** Developing and disseminating narratives that show characters going through a variety of emotions, offering background information, and encouraging empathy.
3. **Role-playing:** Playing out scenarios to gain experience identifying and handling emotions in authentic settings.

Recognizing and Managing Emotions

Identifying and Managing Emotions is to provide autistic children with the tools they need to identify and manage their feelings. Among the strategies are:

1. **Exercises for Self-Reflection:** Helping kids recognize and communicate their feelings by promoting reflection through writing or sketching.

2. **Mindfulness Techniques:**Introduce mindfulness exercises to improve emotional awareness and give yourself the tools you need to control your emotions.

3. **Social Stories:**The creation of social stories that assist kids in recognizing and controlling their emotions in a range of social situations.

Handling Anxiety and Breakdowns

Dealing with emotional storms entails creating plans to steer clear of and lessen the effects of intense feelings. Important components consist of:

1. **Anxiety Reduction Techniques:** To reduce anxiety, use methods like progressive muscle relaxation, deep breathing, or sensory breaks.

2. **Communication strategies:** Making strategies for communication can help people express their needs and feelings in an efficient manner, which will lessen the chance of meltdowns.

3. **Modifying the environment:** Establishing routines and surroundings that are sensory-friendly to reduce triggers that could cause anxiety or meltdowns.

This stage, which is essentially focused on social and emotional development, highlights how critical it is to support autistic children's emotional intelligence. Parents and other caregivers can be crucial in building a foundation of emotional well-being that supports their child's social and emotional development by learning about the nuances of emotions in autism, teaching emotional literacy, assisting with the identification and management of emotions, and dealing with anxiety and meltdowns.

Social Skills and Friendship

This part will focus on friendship and social skills as it continues to examine the social and emotional growth of kids with autism spectrum disorder (ASD). To help people on the autism spectrum develop meaningful social connections, this chapter explores the nuances of friendship-building, social skill-building, and productive peer interaction techniques.

Fostering Companionships

Building Friendships is a Crucial Part of Social and Emotional Development for People with Autism Spectrum Disorder. Understanding the many difficulties that may occur in social situations, parents and other caregivers are essential in helping to create lasting relationships. This includes:

1. **Facilitating Social Opportunities:** This involves creating opportunities for social interaction in organized environments, including playdates, clubs, or group activities.

2. **Promoting Common Interests:** Finding and fostering common interests between peers and people with ASD helps build a bridge of communication.

3. **Encouraging Inclusivity:** Pushing for inclusive behaviors in social settings to make people with ASD feel comfortable and included.

Activities to Develop Social Skills

There are certain activities that enhance social skills and they are a crucial part of the developmental toolset for people with autism spectrum disorders. Purposeful activity development and improvement of social skills are facilitated. Among the strategies are:

1. **Role-playing Scenarios:** By creating scenarios that closely resemble actual social settings, people can hone and improve their social skills.
2. **Group Games:**Playing group games or engaging in activities that promote communication, cooperation, and taking turns.
3. **Communication Workshops:**Enrolling people in communication seminars that emphasize active listening, verbal and nonverbal cues, and other crucial communication skills.

Techniques for Peer Interaction

Helping people with Autism Spectrum Disorder (ASD) navigate social interactions with their peers is made possible by effective peer interaction strategies. Among the strategies are:

1. **Organized Peer Support Programs:** Put in place organized programs in which neurotypical peers are taught to offer assistance and direction.
2. **Visual Supports:**Communication Boards and Social Scripts are examples of visual tools for communication that can be introduced to improve understanding and communication during interactions.

3. **Facilitating Shared Activities:**This is done by Encouraging cooperative initiatives and shared activities that build strong peer relationships.

For people with ASD, friendship and social skills are fundamental parts of their social and emotional fabric. Parents and caregivers enable people with ASD to flourish socially and form meaningful connections by fostering friendships, participating in intentional activities that develop social skills, and putting into practice efficient peer interaction techniques.

Promoting Independence

This phase explores the crucial topic of Promoting Independence in the context of social and emotional development for people with Autism Spectrum Disorder (ASD). It sheds light on the need to develop life skills, support self-advocacy, and put in place efficient adult transition planning to enable people with ASD to become autonomous and self-sufficient.

Development of Life Skills

For people with ASD, developing life skills is a crucial first step on the road to independence. This can accomplished in a number of ways, including :

1. **Activities for Daily Life:** Providing chances for people to practice and become proficient in tasks related to daily life, like meal preparation, personal hygiene, and housework.
2. **Community Navigation:** Organizing activities that improve one's ability to navigate the community, such as going shopping, taking public transportation, and going on social outings.

3. **Task sequencing:** This process allows people to independently finish a variety of tasks by dissecting difficult jobs into manageable steps.

Promoting Advocacy for Oneself

One of the most important ways to support independence for people with ASD is to promote self-advocacy. Among the strategies are:

1. **Communication Training:**Teaching people how to communicate effectively so they can convey their wants, preferences, and objectives is known as communication training.
2. **Posing options for people to make decisions:** Giving people the chance to make decisions about different facets of their lives.
3. **Building Confidence:** Encouraging people to become self-aware and confident to enable them to stand up for themselves in a variety of situations.

Developing an Adult Transition Plan

Transition Planning for Adulthood is a thorough method designed to get people with ASD ready for the opportunities and challenges of adulthood. This includes:

1. **Vocational Training:** Offering instruction and materials to help people build their vocational abilities and choose possible career routes.
2. **Independent Living Skills:**Providing focused assistance to help people develop the skills necessary for independent living, such as

budgeting, finding a place to live, and utilizing neighborhood resources.

3. **Collaborative Goal-creating:** Having conversations about creating goals with people who have ASD, their families, and pertinent support systems.

Essentially, Promoting Independence is a life-changing project that goes beyond the acute difficulties associated with autism and seeks to provide people with ASD with the resources and abilities needed to lead independent and satisfying lives. The development of life skills, self-advocacy, and careful adult transition planning are all ways that parents and caregivers help people with ASD reach their full potential and maintain their autonomy as they work toward independence.

EXERCISES

Recognizing and Managing Emotions:

> Observe your child's emotional expressions and responses in different situations.
> Create a visual chart or use the journal provided to record your child's emotions. Include both positive and challenging moments.

Emotion Management Plan:

> Identify a specific emotion your child may struggle with (e.g., anxiety, frustration).
> Develop a plan to support your child in managing this emotion positively.

Implementation and Adjustments:

> Implement the plan and track its effectiveness over several weeks.
> Adjust the strategy if needed, and celebrate any improvements in your child's emotional well-being.

Chapter six

Collaborating with Healthcare Professionals

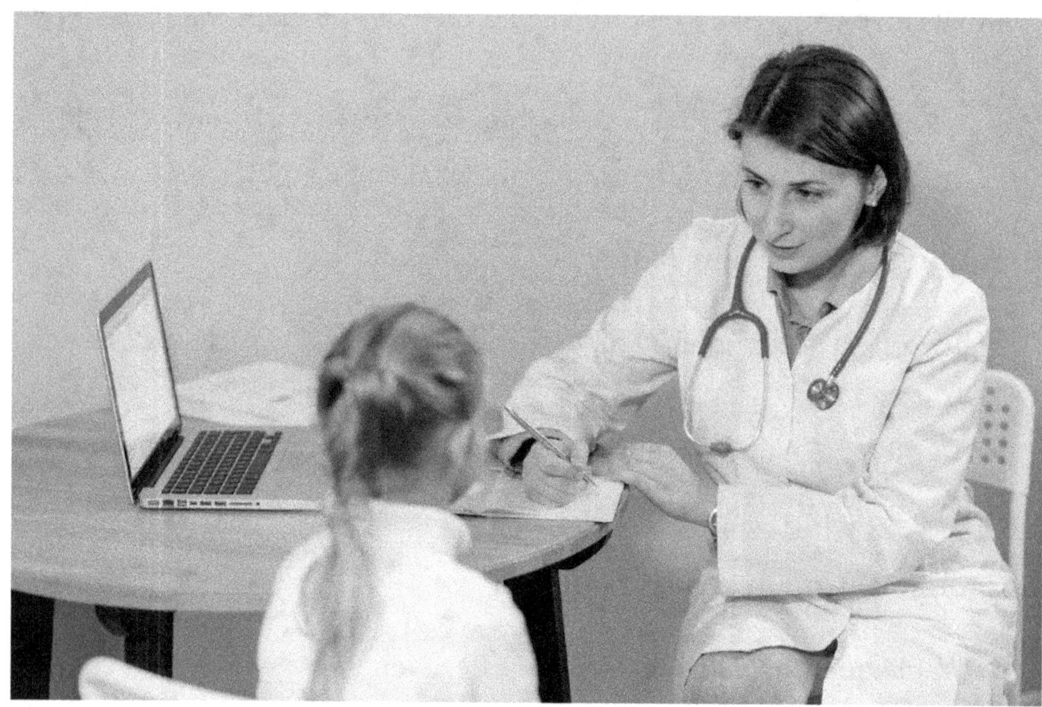

This chapter explores the critical area of Working Together with Healthcare Professionals in the complex world of raising children with Autism Spectrum Disorder (ASD). It will walk readers through the difficult but necessary processes of creating a caring healthcare team, choosing and collaborating with experts, fostering productive relationships with other professionals, and pushing for all-encompassing treatment to guarantee the overall well-being of people with ASD.

Building a Supportive Healthcare Team

Establishing a Supportive Healthcare Team is Essential to Meeting the Varying Needs of People with Autism Spectrum Disorder. This can be done by assembling a group of experts from different fields, such as pediatricians, neurologists, psychologists, occupational therapists, speech therapists, and teachers. Also, collaborative planning which is the process of fostering teamwork and communication to guarantee a cohesive and united approach to patient care.

Choosing and working with experts

Customizing expertise to meet specific needs is essential in Choosing and collaborating with Specialists entails locating experts who have specific knowledge pertinent to the particular requirements of people with ASD. This comprises:

1. **Neurodevelopmental Specialists:** Seeking experts in the field of neurodevelopmental problems to offer thorough evaluations and treatments.
2. **Behavioral therapists:** Working together with behavior analysts and other therapists to address behavioral issues and carry out research-proven treatments.
3. **Communication and Occupational Therapists:**Seeking the assistance of experts in the fields of occupational therapy and communication to solve particular issues in these areas.

Proficiency in Interaction with Experts

Managing collaborative dialogues is a key component of working together, effective communication among professionals guarantees smooth information exchange between caregivers and healthcare providers. This can be done in several ways which includes:

1. **Open Communication Channels:**Clear and transparent channels of communication should be established to exchange aims, concerns, and observations.
2. **Regular Updates:** Giving regular updates on the person's development, difficulties, and any adjustments to their needs.
3. **Listening and Understanding:**Actively listening to expert perspectives and asking for clarification when necessary can help to build a cooperative and knowledgeable partnership.

Promoting All-Inclusive Healthcare

Ensuring holistic well-being involves promoting and defending the overall wellbeing of people with ASD which is a key component of advocating for comprehensive care. Among the strategies are:

1. **Personalized Care Plans:** Creating personalized care plans that take into account a patient's medical, behavioral, educational, and social needs in a collaborative manner.
2. **Coordinating Services:** Promoting coordinated services amongst therapists, educators, and medical professionals to guarantee an integrated and comprehensive approach.

3. Navigating Resources and Insurance: Helping families find resources to support comprehensive care and to navigate the insurance system.

Working together with healthcare professionals is, at its core, a proactive and dynamic process that is essential to the well-being of people with ASD. Through the strategic construction of a supportive healthcare team, the selection of specialists based on individual needs, the promotion of efficient communication, and the advocacy for all-encompassing care, parents and caregivers assume a pivotal role in guaranteeing that their beloveds obtain the customized and varied support necessary for the best possible development and quality of life.

Handling Drugs and Treatments

This part explores the complex world of Managing Medications and Therapies in the complex web of care for people with Autism Spectrum Disorder (ASD). The complex process of comprehending drug options, keeping an eye on their effects, and skillfully incorporating therapy interventions into the everyday lives of people with ASD is examined in this chapter.

Recognizing Your Medication Options

In navigating pharmaceutical possibilities, understanding medication options, pharmacological therapies that are specifically designed to meet the requirements of people with ASD are thoroughly explored. Important things to think about are:

1. **Psychotropic Medications:**Take a closer look at the group of drugs known as psychotropics, which can be used to treat certain conditions including anxiety, OCD, or attention problems.

2. **Antipsychotics and Mood Stabilizers:**Assessing the possible advantages and disadvantages of mood stabilizers and antipsychotic drugs in the treatment of mood disorders or problematic behaviors.

3. **Stimulant Medications:**Examining the function of stimulant drugs in treating attention and hyperactivity problems while weighing the advantages and disadvantages of each.

Tracking the Effects of Medication

Leading the medication journey to maximize treatment, medication effects must be continuously and dynamically monitored. This includes:

1. **Frequent Medical Reviews:** Arranging for routine medical examinations with medical specialists to evaluate how a person's drugs are affecting their general health.

2. **Monitoring Behavioral Changes:** Keeping track of how behavior, emotions, and attention vary to see any possible adverse consequences or necessary corrections.

3. **Collaborative Decision-Making:**Working together with medical professionals to change prescriptions, modify dosages, or consider other choices in light of the patient's response is known as collaborative decision-making.

Including Therapies in Everyday Activities

Smooth integration of supportive interventions including different therapeutic interventions into daily life entails integrating therapies into people with ASD's daily routine in a smooth manner. This comprises:

1. **Consistency in Therapeutic Approaches:**Ensuring that therapeutic interventions, such as occupational therapy, behavioral therapy, and speech and language therapy, are applied consistently throughout daily activities is known as consistency in therapeutic approaches.

2. **Home-Based Strategies:** Adapting therapy techniques for use in the family setting, encouraging consistency between outside treatment and everyday activities.

3. **Cooperation with Therapists:** Creating individualized and attainable goals for everyday tasks through cooperative work with therapists.

Managing medications and therapies is essentially a delicate process involving scientific knowledge, close observation, and deliberate integration into the day-to-day activities of people with ASD. Caregivers and healthcare professionals can work together to navigate the complex terrain of interventions, aiming for a balanced and personalized approach that maximizes the well-being and developmental progress of individuals with ASD, by thoroughly understanding medication options, closely monitoring their effects, and seamlessly integrating therapies into daily routines.

Using Financial and Insurance Resources

Fostering financial well-being for comprehensive care is explored in the crucial topic of Insurance and Financial Resource Navigation in the continuous process of providing care for people with Autism Spectrum Disorder (ASD). To promote financial well-being and guarantee comprehensive care for people with ASD, this chapter offers insights on obtaining insurance coverage, investigating financial support programs, and lobbying for legislative changes.

Getting Insurance Protection

Unlocking Financial Support with Insurance coverage is a critical step in getting the funds needed for the variety of needs of people with autism spectrum disorder. Among the strategies are:

1. **Comprehending Policy Coverage:** Examining insurance plans in detail to understand what treatments, prescription drugs, and medical interventions are covered.

2. **Making Use of Benefits Particular to Autism:** Determining and making use of benefits particular to autism-related interventions, such as behavioral therapy and expert consultations.

3. **Sustaining Frequent Communication:** Maintaining open lines of communication with insurance companies to ask questions about specifics of coverage, submit claims, and resolve any inconsistencies.

Examining Programs for Financial Assistance

Researching Financial Assistance Programs entails locating and utilizing a range of financial support sources. This comprises:

1. **Government Assistance Programs:** looking into and submitting applications for government-sponsored initiatives like Medicaid and Supplemental Security Income (SSI) that offer financial aid to people with disabilities.

2. **Nonprofit Organizations:** Seeking assistance from foundations and nonprofit groups that provide grants or other financial aid, especially for people with ASD and their families.

3. **Community Resources:**Using available community resources in the area to help pay for counseling, educational initiatives, or other necessary services.

Making the Case for Policy Changes

Promoting Policy Changes entails actively taking part in initiatives to create laws that improve accessibility and financial assistance for people with ASD. Among the strategies are:

1. **Participating in Advocacy Groups:** Becoming a member of or lending assistance to advocacy groups that work to reform local, state, or federal laws about autism.

2. **Interacting with Lawmakers:** Reaching out to politicians to discuss issues, offer firsthand accounts of difficulties encountered, and promote laws that cater to the special requirements of people with ASD.

3. **Participating in Public Forums:**Attending town halls, public forums, or policy talks can help build inclusive policies by providing firsthand viewpoints and thoughts.

Navigating Insurance and Financial Resources is essentially a proactive, multi-pronged endeavor to guarantee that financial concerns do not become impediments to providing individuals with ASD with comprehensive care. Through securing insurance, looking into financial aid options, and lobbying for legislative reforms, caregivers and ASD sufferers take on the role of advocates not just for their own urgent needs but also for systemic advancements that benefit the larger autism community.

EXERCISES

Building a Supportive Healthcare Team:

- ➤ Reflect on your experiences collaborating with healthcare professionals. What aspects have been positive, and where do you see opportunities for improvement?
- ➤ List any specialists you currently work with or would like to explore for additional support.

Effective Communication:

- ➤ Describe a situation where effective communication with a healthcare professional positively impacted your child's care.
- ➤ Share one communication strategy you find particularly useful when interacting with healthcare professionals.

Advocacy for Comprehensive Care:

- ➤ Consider a time when you advocated for comprehensive care for your child. What challenges did you face, and what were the outcomes?
- ➤ List three key components you believe are essential for comprehensive care in the context of autism.

Chapter seven

Addressing Behavioral Challenges

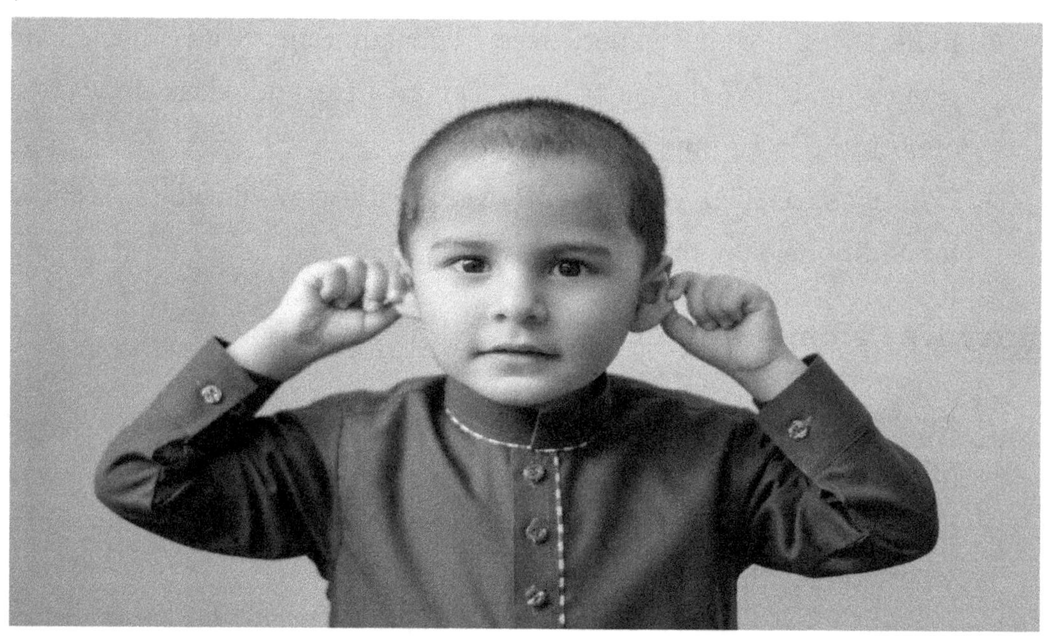

This phase of the complex process of raising children with autism spectrum disorder (ASD) explores the subtle world of dealing with behavioral challenges. To promote positive growth and solve behavioral issues for people with ASD, this chapter explains how to apply Positive Behavior Support, use behavior analysis principles, create efficient behavior plans, and use reinforcement tactics.

Positive Behavior Support

The philosophy of Positive Behavior Support serves as a roadmap for handling behavioral issues, placing special emphasis on proactive tactics that encourage positive behaviors and improve the general well-being of people with ASD.

Fundamentals of Behavior Analysis

An Understanding of Behavioral Dynamics A core understanding of the dynamics governing behavior is provided by principles. Important ideas consist of:

1. **ABC analysis:** This is the process of examining causes, effects, and patterns to spot trends and comprehend the variables affecting behavior.
2. **Functional Behavior Assessment (FBA):** FBAs are used to determine the reason or function of a behavior, which helps in the creation of successful interventions.
3. **Setting Events and Motivating Operations:**Identifying internal and external factors that affect the probability and intensity of behaviors.

Crafting Useful Behavior Plans

Customizing approaches for achieving and formulating successful behavior plans entails creating unique approaches to deal with certain behavioral issues. This comprises:

1. **Clear Behavior Definitions:** Defining target behaviors precisely in terms of what can be observed and measured will help to ensure that the goals of the intervention are understood.

2. **Setting Achievable and Realistic Goals:** Taking into account the skills and developmental stage of the individual, realistic goals should be set for behavior modification.

3. **Collaborative Planning:** To guarantee consistency and efficacy of behavior programs, involve parents, caregivers, educators, and other professionals in the planning process.

Techniques for Reinforcement

Consistency Strategies are essential for decreasing the incidence of problematic behaviors and for molding and rewarding desirable behaviors. Among the procedures are:

1. **Positive reinforcement:** this involves the process of making desired behaviors more likely by bestowing benefits, accolades, or privileges.

2. **Token Systems:** Putting in place economies based on tokens, in which people receive tokens for good deeds and can swap them for prizes.

3. **Natural Reinforces:** To encourage positive actions, recognize and use naturally occurring reinforces in the surroundings.

Essentially, Positive Behavior Support is emphasized as a guiding philosophy in this chapter, Addressing Behavioral Challenges. Through comprehension of behavior analysis principles, creation of efficient behavior plans, and application of reinforcement strategies, caregivers and professionals establish a nurturing atmosphere that promotes positive growth, reduces obstacles, and improves the general quality of life for individuals diagnosed with ASD.

Coping with Difficult Behaviors

This concept examines handling challenging behaviors in the complex context of resolving behavioral challenges in autism spectrum disorder (ASD). To effectively support behavior for people with ASD, this chapter explores the role of behaviors, crisis intervention strategies, and the cooperative role of professionals.

Recognizing the Purpose of Behaviors

Behavior is a potent means of communication for people with autism spectrum disorder (ASD). Every action, no matter how constructive or difficult, reveals something about the person's needs, feelings, or surroundings. Deciphering these signals and creating therapies that work requires an understanding of the function of behaviors. An extensive examination of this key idea is provided below:

1. Assessment of Functional Behavior:

The procedure of carrying out a Functional Behavior Assessment (FBA) is fundamental to comprehending how behaviors function. This methodical technique entails:

- **Observation:** Paying close attention to and recording the actions, outcomes, and antecedents (triggers) connected to certain circumstances.
- **Data collection:** Gathering information over time to spot behavioral patterns and trends that allow for a thorough study.

- **Interviews and surveys:** Information is gathered from the person, teachers, and caregivers to provide context and possible reasons for behavior.

2. Communicative Nature of Behaviors:

People with ASD frequently use challenging behaviors as a form of communication. Typical communication tasks consist of:

- **Expressing Needs:** Certain behaviors can indicate that a person needs comfort, attention, sensory stimulation, or help to achieve a desire.
- **Communicating Discomfort:** Several behaviors, including those related to pain, sensory overload, or environmental aversions, may be signs of physical discomfort.
- **Expression of Emotions:** When people find it difficult to express themselves verbally, their actions might reveal their happiness, displeasure, or anxiety.

3. Environmental Triggers:

Understanding the reasons behind specific behaviors requires an identification of environmental triggers. Some examples of triggers are:

- **Sensory Overload:**Overstimulation resulting from sensory inputs like bright lights, loud noises, or crowded areas is known as sensory overload.

- **Routine Changes:** Anxiety and difficult behaviors can be significantly triggered by changes to established routines.
- **Unmet Needs:** When a person's basic needs—such as hunger or exhaustion—are not met, it may cause them to act in ways that try to satisfy them.

4. Individualized Factors:

It's critical to acknowledge how highly individualized behavior is in its function. A communication strategy that is effective for one person may not be for another. Among the variables affecting how behavior functions are:

- **Developmental Stage:** A behavior may correspond with a certain developmental stage or be developmentally appropriate.
- **Cognitive Abilities:** The selection of therapies is guided by an understanding of the patient's cognitive abilities and processing preferences.
- **Social Context:** Taking into account the dynamics and social context of an individual can offer important insights into the purposes of their acts.

5. Implications for Intervention:

Developing focused and successful interventions is aided by an understanding of how behaviors function.

- **Function-Based Interventions:** Developing treatment plans that take into account the behavior's recognized function while tackling its underlying causes.

- **Teaching Alternative Behaviors:** Presenting socially acceptable substitutes for problematic behaviors that serve the same purpose.

- **Environmental Modifications:** Changing the surroundings to reduce stressors and establish a setting that encourages constructive conduct.

In summary, deciphering the purpose of behaviors in people with ASD is a complex and ever-changing process. It calls for close observation, teamwork with experts, and a dedication to providing tailored help. Caregivers and experts can apply tactics that address the underlying needs, encourage positive alternatives, and improve the general well-being of individuals with ASD by understanding the messages hidden beneath actions.

Techniques for Crisis Intervention

The use of crisis intervention techniques is essential for managing and defusing difficult circumstances involving people with autism spectrum disorder (ASD). These methods are meant to protect the person receiving care, the caregivers, and other people involved. This is a thorough summary of crisis response strategies designed specifically for people with ASD:

1. Techniques for De-escalation:

- **Keep Calm:** Try not to raise the person's stress levels by acting in a tense manner.

- **Non-Threatening Posture:** Maintain a relaxed, open stance while averting direct eye contact.
- **Use Calm Tone:** To reassure the person and prevent upsetting them, speak in a soothing tone.

2. Preparing for Safety:

- **Preventive Measures:** These actions should be taken, such as getting rid of potentially harmful items or setting up a secure area.
- **Emergency Contacts:** Make sure your emergency contact information is easily accessible so you can get in touch with experts or support systems right away.
- **Clear Exits:** If an evacuation is required, locate and keep clear exits to enable a quick and secure departure.

3. Communication in an Emergency:

- **Simple Instructions:** Clearly state what has to be done and break it down into manageable steps.
- **Visual Aids:** To improve comprehension, make use of visual aids like cue cards or schedules.
- **Use of Technology:** During times of crisis, use technology to help in communication. Examples of this include communication apps and visual assistance on tablets.

4. Engaging Methods:

- **Give Them Options:** Giving the person options will help them feel more in charge and independent.

- **Preferred Activities:** To refocus attention and reduce anxiety, provide favored hobbies or objects.
- **Sensory Comfort:** Provide products that promote sensory comfort, such as relaxing pastimes or fidget toys.

To put it briefly, this phase on Coping with Challenging Behaviors emphasizes the significance of comprehending the purpose of behaviors, utilizing crisis intervention strategies, and working with experts to provide all-encompassing behavior assistance. Individuals with ASD are empowered to effectively traverse challenges and promote positive behavioral outcomes by caregivers and support networks, who also help them understand the communicative side of behaviors, handle crisis moments with care, and build a cohesive approach with experts.

Encouraging Self-Regulation

Empowering People with Autism Spectrum Disorder (ASD) addresses self-regulation as a means of overcoming behavioral difficulties. This chapter explains how to help people with ASD learn self-calming techniques, build coping mechanisms, and establish a secure environment for regulation so they can become more adept at controlling their emotions and behaviors.

Passing along Self-Calming Techniques

Teaching Self-Calming Strategies entails giving people with ASD a toolkit of methods for controlling their emotional arousal and sensory perception. Among the strategies are:

- **Deep Breathing:** Leading people through deep breathing techniques to ease tension and encourage relaxation.
- **Visual aids:** To help with self-regulation, introduce visual aids like schedules or calm-down charts.

Developing Coping Skills

Creating Coping Skills is a proactive strategy to help people with ASD face the obstacles of daily living. This includes:

- **Problem Solving Strategies:**Teaching strategies for resolving disagreements and problems so that students can handle them on their own.
- **Emotional Expression:**Healthy emotional expression through spoken words, visual arts, or written words is encouraged.
- **Social scripts:** a set of words or phrases that people can use to express their emotions in appropriate social contexts.

Establishing a Secure Environment for Law

Creating Zones of Comfort entails designing settings that support a person's emotional and sensory needs. Among the strategies are:

- **Sensory-Friendly Design:**Designing a setting with minimal sensory triggers in mind, such as by reducing noise or using soft lighting, is known as sensory-friendly design.
- **Comfort things:** To create a feeling of security, provide comfort things like pillows, blankets, and weighted blankets.

- Customized Retreats: Setting aside particular locations as places for people to withdraw when they're feeling overwhelmed.

Essentially, the focus of this phase on Promoting Self-Regulation is on giving people with ASD the tools they need to actively control their emotions and behaviors. Caregivers and support networks enhance an individual's autonomy, resilience, and general well-being by imparting self-calming techniques, helping them develop coping mechanisms, and setting up safe areas for regulation.

EXERCISES

Positive Behavior Support:

- ➤ Share an instance where positive behavior support was effective in managing a challenging behavior.
- ➤ Describe the development of an effective behavior plan for your child.

Understanding the Function of Behaviors:

- ➤ Choose a specific behavior your child exhibits. Reflect on the possible functions of that behavior.
- ➤ Document any insights gained from understanding the function of your child's behaviors.

Coping with Challenging Behaviors:

- ➤ Recall a challenging behavior situation and describe how you applied crisis intervention techniques.
- ➤ Share your experience collaborating with professionals for behavior support.

Promoting Self-Regulation:

- ➤ Document the effectiveness of teaching self-calming strategies for your child.
- ➤ Identify situations where creating a safe space for regulation has been beneficial.

Chapter eight

Family Dynamics and Siblings

This chapter delves into the complex dynamics of siblings and family dynamics, revealing the subtleties that weave together the lives of families with children who have autism spectrum disorder (ASD). This chapter is a tapestry that deftly navigates the subject of supporting siblings, investigating the dynamics and relationships between them, addressing potential problems, and purposefully fostering the ties that bind them.

Supporting Siblings

Assisting Siblings requires a conscious attempt to recognize and negotiate the unique experiences and difficulties that siblings of people with ASD invariably face. The aim is to foster a comprehensive and encouraging family atmosphere.

Dynamics and Relationships between Siblings

Untangling the Threads of Sibling Connections explores the complex network of interactions and experiences that siblings of people with ASD manage. Important elements consist of:

1. **Appreciating Differences:**Encouraging siblings to embrace and respect their brother or sister with ASD's distinctive features rather than just tolerating them is known as "appreciating differences."
2. **Defining family duties:** Engaging in dialogue to clarify duties within the family while highlighting the important contributions made by each sibling.
3. **Cultivating Empathy:** Creating a profound understanding and connection by shedding light on the difficulties their brother with ASD faces.

Handling Sibling Issues

Creating a forum where siblings can freely share their ideas, concerns, and questions is part of Building Bridges via Open Communication. This encompasses:

1. **Family Conclaves:** Arranging family get-togethers as a platform for siblings to freely discuss their experiences and voice any concerns.

2. **Heart-to-Hearts:** Setting aside time for one-on-one conversations with each sibling to delve into their unique issues and feelings.

3. **Expert Advice:** Including family therapists or mental health specialists when necessary to assist in resolving difficult feelings and issues.

Encouraging the Bond between Siblings

|Fostering sibling bonding emphasizes how crucial it is to develop strong bonds between siblings. Strategies include:

1. **Shared Pursuits:**Encourage common interests and pastimes that not only strengthen sibling bonds but also serve as a storehouse of happy memories.

2. **Knowledge Empowerment:** Providing developmentally appropriate information on ASD to improve understanding and reduce apprehension.

3. **Honoring Milestones:** Recognizing and honoring the significant and small accomplishments of every sibling in the family.

Essentially, the goal of this chapter on Siblings and Family Dynamics is to create a loving environment in which each family member—including the siblings—feels accepted, understood, and valued. Families can strengthen their bonds and lay a solid foundation for the holistic development and well-being of every family member, including those with ASD, by understanding sibling relationships and dynamics, addressing concerns with empathy and open communication, and actively fostering sibling bonding through shared experiences and joyous occasions.

Collaboration and Communication within the Family

This explores the essential elements of Family Communication and Collaboration within the complex fabric of family life. This chapter examines the value of candid communication, group decision-making, and the skillful juggling of each family member's particular demands.

Honest Dialogue within the Family

Understanding, empathy, and harmony within the family are based on open communication. This includes:

1. **Regular Family meetings:** This should be held regularly to promote an open environment and give everyone a voice.
2. **Active Listening:** Family members should be encouraged to actively listen to one another's viewpoints to foster sincere understanding.
3. **Establishing Safe Spaces:** Setting aside areas where family members can freely express their sentiments without fear of repercussions.

Situation:

One family member says during a meeting that they are feeling overpowered by the difficulties of helping a sibling with ASD. The family can talk about and exchange ideas for allocating responsibilities and offering emotional support because of open communication.

Shared Decision-Making

Shared Decision-Making calls for the participation of all family members in decisions that affect the entire family. Among the strategies are:

1. **Building Consensus:** Making an effort to come to a resolution in which all viewpoints are taken into account.
2. **Transparent Communication:** Building trust within the family by giving clear and transparent information about decisions that need to be taken.
3. **Inclusive Problem Solving:** Working together to solve problems and transforming obstacles into chances for group development.

Situation:

Taking into account the kid's special needs and the opinions of all family members, the family decides on the best therapy method for their child with ASD.

Balancing the Needs of Each Family Member

Harmonizing the demands and needs of each family member entails identifying and attending to each member's particular demands. This comprises:

1. **Customized Support Plans:** Creating plans that are adapted to each family member's unique requirements, including those of individuals with ASD.
2. **Adaptability and Flexibility:** Being adaptable to changing conditions and demands.
3. **Making Self-Care a Priority:** To preserve each family member's general well-being, self-care habits should be encouraged.

Situation:

With therapy sessions, school commitments, and work responsibilities, the family manages a hectic week. Their cooperative planning and responsibilities ensure that every family member's requirements are taken into account.

Family Communication and Collaboration, in its simplest form, aims to establish a family culture in which candid communication is valued, choices are made jointly, and the various needs of each family member are acknowledged and harmoniously balanced. This chapter seeks to assist families in fostering a cohesive and encouraging atmosphere where each person's voice is respected and heard by using real-world scenarios and doable tactics.

Parental Resilience and Self-Care

This part explores the vital components of resilience and self-care for parents within the complex fabric of family life. This chapter delves into the skill of identifying and handling parental stress, the significance of giving self-care priority, and the priceless function of creating a network of support.

Identifying and Handling the Stress of Parenting

Identifying and Managing Parental Stress is a Fundamental Step in Encouraging Resilience. This includes:

1. **Self-Reflection:** Encouraging parents to reflect on their lives and pinpoint their stressors.
2. **Stress Management Strategies:** Teaching parents useful stress-reduction strategies including mindfulness, deep breathing, and scheduled pauses.
3. **Professional Support:** Promoting the idea that when stress gets too much, one should seek professional assistance.

Situation:

A parent who notices their child is more stressed during difficult behavioral episodes asks a therapist for advice on how to create healthy coping mechanisms.

Giving Self-Care Priority

Prioritizing Self-Care highlights how important it is for parents to make conscious decisions about their health. Among the strategies are:

1. **Creating limits:** Clearly defining the limits between personal time and caregiving obligations.

2. **Hobbies:** Encouraging parents to partake in their favorite pastimes as a way to unwind.

3. **Frequent Check-Ins:** Making sure self-care routines continue by regularly evaluating oneself.

Situation:

A parent sets aside time each week for a personal activity. A creative outlet provides them with comfort and renewal away from their caring responsibilities.

Establishing a Helpful Network

Developing a Supportive Network entails establishing relationships with others who are cognizant of and sympathetic to the particular difficulties that parents encounter. This comprises:

1. **Community Involvement:** Taking part in online or local parent communities with like-minded individuals.

2. **Reciprocal Relationships:** Building connections based on reciprocity in which parents lend support to one another.

3. **Professional Guidance:** To manage emotional difficulties, seek advice from therapists, support groups, or counselors.

Situation:

Parents join a local support group for families with children diagnosed with autism spectrum disorders (ASD), forming a network wherein experiences are exchanged and support from one another becomes an invaluable asset.

Essentially, the goal of this phase on Resilience and Self-Care for Parents is to strengthen parents' internal foundations of strength. Parents can resiliently negotiate the challenges of raising a child with ASD by recognizing and managing stress, prioritizing self-care, and developing a support network. This allows parents to maintain their well-being as a top priority within the complex fabric of family life.

EXERCISES

Supporting Siblings:

> Reflect on your efforts to support siblings. What unique challenges have you encountered?

> Share positive experiences fostering sibling bonding and relationships.

Family Communication and Collaboration:

> Evaluate the effectiveness of open communication within your family. What strategies enhance family communication?

> Describe a shared decision-making process that positively impacted your family dynamics.

Resilience and Self-Care for Parents:

> Recognize a moment when you successfully managed parental stress. What strategies did you employ?

> Outline your self-care priorities and how you have built a supportive network.

Chapter nine

Planning for the Future

This chapter will take you on a journey through the important stage of planning for the future that affects people with autism spectrum disorder (ASD) and their families. The strategic elements of transition planning are discussed in this chapter, including the creation of transition goals, job training, and the development of independent living abilities.

Transition Planning

Bridging the Gap to Adulthood is done thorough procedure called transition planning, it is intended to assist people with ASD in making the move from adolescence to adulthood. This procedure comprises:

Formulating Transitional Objectives

Creating Transition Goals entails working together to establish goals that will enable a smooth transition. Among the strategies are:

1. **Person-Centered Planning:** Creating objectives that are in line with each person's preferences, strengths, and ambitions.
2. **Including Stakeholders:** Involving the person, their family, teachers, and other pertinent experts in the process of defining goals.
3. **Long-Term and Short-Term Goals:** Setting both realistic short-term objectives and long-term aspirations will help to ensure a smooth transition.

Speech therapy and workplace communication seminars are used to help an individual with ASD achieve a transition objective of developing good communication skills for the workplace.

Opportunities and Vocational Training

The goals of vocational training and opportunities are to help people become independent and find fulfilling work while also preparing them for the workforce. This comprises:

1. **Talents assessment:** determining a person's talents and using them to investigate potential career pathways.
2. **Skill development:** This is done by providing specialized training to improve job-specific competencies and skills.
3. **Investigating Career Paths:** Working with career counselors to investigate a variety of job alternatives that fit the person's interests.

A person who is interested in technology-related professions enrolls in a computer programming-focused vocational training program.

Capabilities for Independent Living

To enable people with ASD to manage daily life independently, independent living skills are crucial. This includes:

1. **Daily Living Tasks:**Teaching basic daily living skills like cleaning, cooking, and personal hygiene.
2. **Financial Literacy:**Teaching people how to manage their money, create a budget, and make wise financial decisions is known as financial literacy.
3. **Community Engagement:** Creating avenues for community involvement to improve integration and social skills.

A young adult with autism spectrum disorder (ASD) can take part in a program that teaches them how to live independently by managing their money, grocery shopping, and taking public transit.

For people with ASD and their families, Planning for the Future essentially serves as a road map, helping them navigate the important transition to adulthood. This chapter seeks to enable people with ASD to enjoy satisfied, independent lives in the years to come by helping them create transition goals, investigating opportunities for vocational training, and learning independent living skills.

Financial and Legal Arrangements

An important part of getting ready for the future for people with autism spectrum disorder (ASD) is legal and financial planning, which is covered in this section. The complexities of guardianship and alternatives, special needs trusts, and obtaining public assistance are covered in detail in this chapter.

Alternatives to Guardianship

As individuals with ASD enter adulthood, guardianship and alternatives must make arrangements for their continued care and decision-making. Important things to think about are:

1. **Guardianship Options:**Examining several guardianship arrangements, such as supported decision-making, restricted guardianship, and full guardianship.

2. **Alternatives to Guardianship:**Examining less restrictive options such as healthcare proxies, powers of attorney, or supported decision-making agreements as substitutes for guardianship.

3. **Legal Procedures:** Being aware of the legal steps necessary to set up guardianship or other alternative arrangements.

Special NeedsTrusts

: When it comes to inheritance, settlements, or donations, Special Needs Trusts are essential for ensuring the financial stability of people with Autism Spectrum Disorder. Important elements consist of:

1. **Creating Trusts:** Creating trusts with the express purpose of attending to the special requirements of people with disabilities.
2. **Maintaining Eligibility:** Making sure the trust is set up to maintain eligibility for government support initiatives.
3. **Professional Guidance:**Seeking professional guidance from attorneys and financial advisors with knowledge of special needs planning.

Getting Government Assistance

Navigating support systems is one of the ways to get government benefits, one must be aware of and make use of the several support programs that are accessible to people with ASD. This comprises:

1. **Program Research:** This involves locating and learning about government benefits including Medicaid, SSI, and vocational rehabilitation services.
2. **Eligibility Criteria:**A thorough understanding of the requirements for each program and adherence to them are necessary for qualifying.
3. **Application Procedures:** Handling the government benefit application procedures, which frequently require paperwork and supporting evidence.

Legal and Financial Planning serves as a manual for strengthening the stability of people with ASD in the future. This chapter has explored guardianship and alternatives, special needs trusts, and government benefit access to enable families to make well-informed decisions that protect the legal rights and financial stability of their adult-adjusted loved ones with ASD.

Campaigning for Acceptance and Inclusion

The focus here is to highlight the need to ensure that people with Autism Spectrum Disorder (ASD) are accepted, included, and supported in their communities. It also advocates the value of championing equal opportunities. This chapter explores tactics for advocating locally and nationally and encouraging community inclusion.

Fostering Inclusion in the Community

Encouraging Community Inclusion entails developing settings that encourage the engagement and acceptance of people with ASD. Important components consist of:

1. **Education and Awareness:** Debunking myths and fostering understanding, involves increasing community awareness about ASD.
2. **Working Together with Community Entities:** Creating inclusive possibilities through interacting with local companies, schools, and community organizations.
3. **Community Activities:** Organizing gatherings and exercises that promote involvement and a feeling of community among people with ASD.

Local and Nationwide Advocacy

Local and national levels advocacy entails actively pursuing societal and policy changes that support the acceptance and rights of people with ASD. Among the strategies are:

1. **Interaction with Local Authorities:** Working together to promote inclusive policies with local government agencies, educational institutions, and healthcare providers.
2. **Engaging in Advocacy Groups:** Becoming a member of or starting advocacy groups that aim to advance the rights of people with autism spectrum disorders on a larger scale.
3. **Legislative Advocacy:** Taking part in campaigns and legislative procedures to influence laws and policies that promote tolerance and acceptance.

To put it simply, this section on Advocacy for Inclusion and Acceptance is a call to action, imploring people to actively fight for the acceptance and rights of people with ASD on a personal, family, and community level. This chapter seeks to create a society in which people with ASD can flourish, be accepted, and fully engage in all facets of community life by encouraging community inclusion and taking part in advocacy initiatives at the local and national levels.

Changing How the Public Views Autism

To create a culture that accepts and supports people on the autistic spectrum, public perception of autism is essential. Myths and misconceptions about autism must be debunked to properly shape this perspective. The first approach is to show autism as a spectrum disorder rather than a condition that suits all people. We can dispel myths and advance a more realistic knowledge of the spectrum by highlighting the many talents, strengths, and distinctive characteristics of people with autism.

A crucial element in molding public opinion is stressing the importance of neurodiversity. Providing examples of autism within the larger context of human neurodiversity promotes acceptance of neurological variations. This paradigm change encourages society to see autism as a normal variance in people's experiences of the world rather than as a deficiency or disorder. Public awareness of this variety can be raised by using illustrative campaigns and materials, which can show off the distinct viewpoints and contributions of people with autism.

Campaigns for public awareness are also essential in influencing perception. Empathy and understanding are cultivated through providing examples of the everyday struggles experienced by people with autism and their families. Personal accounts, whether in the form of books, films, or other visual media, can offer striking examples of the successes and setbacks faced by the autistic community. These initiatives have the potential to humanize the lives of people with autism and make the public more understanding and knowledgeable.

Education is also a powerful instrument for influencing perception. It is possible to dispel stereotypes by providing examples of how inclusive education, employment opportunities, and community integration are crucial for people with autism. Workshops, seminars, and inclusive instructional resources can be effective means of demonstrating the advantages of accepting neurodiversity within different social contexts. People may dismantle obstacles and change public perceptions about autism when they experience the benefits of inclusion.

The last component in influencing public opinion is community participation. Demonstrating how people with autism actively participate in and contribute to a variety of community activities aids in dispelling the myth that people with autism are socially isolated. Events, programs, and efforts that promote inclusivity can provide concrete examples of the value that neurodiversity adds to society.

In conclusion, influencing how the general public views autism necessitates a multimodal strategy that makes use of images in a variety of formats. Through exhibiting the variety, capabilities, and day-to-day encounters of people with autism spectrum disorders, we may dispel misconceptions, promote comprehension, and construct a more tolerant and inclusive community. We can progressively change public perceptions of autism by educating the public, running awareness campaigns, and involving the community. This will help us create a society in which people with autism are respected for their distinctive contributions.

EXERCISES

Transition Planning:

- ➤ Develop specific transition goals for your child. What aspirations do you have for their future?
- ➤ Reflect on the challenges and successes you've encountered in developing transition goals.

Legal and Financial Planning:

- ➤ Evaluate your understanding of guardianship and alternatives. How have you approached legal and financial planning for your child's future?
- ➤ Outline the steps you've taken or plan to take in creating a special needs trust.

Advocacy for Inclusion and Acceptance:

- ➤ Describe your efforts in promoting community inclusion. How have you advocated at local and national levels?
- ➤ Share an instance where you successfully advocated for a more inclusive environment.

Chapter ten

Celebrating Milestones and Successes

This chapter bears witness to the significance of recognizing and honoring the accomplishments of people with autism spectrum disorder (ASD) and their families. It offers a journey reflection, highlighting the importance of acknowledging advancement, recording significant events, and commemorating individual development and achievements.

Reflecting on Progress

The chapter starts by urging people to evaluate their accomplishments and the networks of people that support them. This includes:

Recording Significant Events

Documenting milestones is a practice of recording and preserving significant achievements and developmental strides. Strategies include :

1. **Maintaining diaries:**Encouraging people, caregivers, and educators to keep diaries or logs that emphasize significant occasions and achievements.
2. **Visual documentation:** Thisis the process of designating significant events with the use of visual aids like pictures, movies, or creative depictions.

Identifying Individual Development

Acknowledging Personal Growth entails recognizing the person's advancement and enhanced capacities. This comprises:

1. **Self-Reflection:** Encouraging people to consider how they have grown personally, acknowledging the challenges they have faced and the abilities they have earned.
2. **Feedback and Validation:** To strengthen the feeling of achievement, offer both constructive criticism and encouraging remarks.

Highlighting Success

Celebrating Achievements highlights how important it is to joyfully recognize successes. This includes:

1. **Family and Community Involvement:** Joining friends, family, and neighbors in festivities to build a network of support.
2. **Ceremonial activities:** Planning celebrations or activities to commemorate important anniversaries, encouraging pride in the community.

This section serves as a reminder that there are many minor and large successes along the way of living with autism. Through introspection, goal-setting, acknowledging personal development, and commemorating accomplishments, people with ASD and those who support them can craft a positive story that highlights resiliency, perseverance, and the value of every step forward. This chapter is an appeal to value the accomplishments that support the overall growth and well-being of people on the autism spectrum and to appreciate the individuality of every journey.

Building a Brilliant Future

This crucial section focuses on creating the foundation for a vibrant and meaningful future for people with autism spectrum disorder (ASD), rather than just acknowledging past successes. This chapter aims to carefully mold a trajectory of ongoing improvement and personal development by delving into the ideas of promoting independence, lifelong learning, and adopting a positive mindset.

Promoting Lifelong Education

Encouraging Lifelong Learning acknowledges that education is a continuous, flexible process rather than a finished product. It entails establishing an atmosphere that actively fosters intellectual curiosity in people with ASD, rather than just supporting it. This includes promoting career training, experiential learning, and self-directed exploration in addition to conventional school courses. People are better prepared to take on new challenges, explore personal interests, and realize their full potential at all stages of life when a culture of lifelong learning is fostered.

Fostering Self-reliance

One of the main tactics for giving people with ASD a bright future is fostering independence. This comprehensive strategy entails giving people the assistance and resources they need to acquire critical life skills. The focus is on developing autonomy, from doing everyday living tasks to taking part in decision-making. This approach adjusts assistance based on each person's needs, progressively increasing responsibility as people advance. In doing so, a feeling of resilience and self-efficacy is fostered, laying the groundwork for a future characterized by individual autonomy, self-sufficiency, and an improved standard of living.

Taking a Positive Viewpoint

Adopting a Positive Outlook is a way of thinking that affects not just the person but also the larger community. It entails developing an outlook that sees opportunities rather than constraints. This mindset is based on appreciating all accomplishments, no matter how minor, and seeing obstacles as chances for personal development. It entails using a strengths-based approach and redefining failures as worthwhile teaching moments. By doing this, people with ASD not only become resilient and gain a sense of purpose in life, but they also have an impact on how the community views and supports them. This change helps to build a welcoming and encouraging environment that helps people with ASD move toward a bright future.

Building a Bright Future for your child is essentially a thorough examination of the approaches and ideologies that support the long-term development of people with ASD. Through the establishment of a positive mindset that permeates the community, the promotion of self-sufficiency through customized support, the instillation of a love of learning, and the creation of a resilient and self-assured future, this chapter aims to enable people with ASD to embrace their paths.

Creating a Community of Support

In this section the importance of community is discussed in people with autism spectrum disorder (ASD). The focus is on creating an atmosphere that actively works to create a supportive community while also aggressively acknowledging the special requirements of people with ASD. The tactic of participating in community activities as a way to build relationships and encourage inclusivity is examined in this chapter.

Taking Part in Local Events

One tactic to promote the active engagement and participation of people with ASD in their communities is to get involved in community events. This includes:

1. **Event Planning:**Including people with ASD actively in the preparation and coordination of community events to guarantee that their comfort and preferences are taken into account is known as inclusive event planning.

2. **Events Tailored to Diverse Interests:** Offering a wide range of events that appeal to different interests enables people with ASD to select activities that they find meaningful.

3. **Offering Sensory-Friendly Options:** Reducing sensory overload and offering quiet areas for anyone who might need a break will help make community activities more sensory-friendly.

People with ASD can strengthen their social skills, sense of community, and sense of interaction by taking part in community events. It also fosters acceptance and appreciation of neurodiversity and provides a forum for community members to learn more about ASD.

This section is essentially a thorough investigation of how participating actively in community events might help foster an atmosphere that is supportive of people with ASD. Communities may become places where people with ASD feel appreciated, connected, and essential to the social fabric by embracing inclusivity in event planning, accommodating a range of interests, and offering sensory-friendly options.

EXERCISES

Reflecting on Progress:

> ➤ Document specific milestones your child has achieved. How have these milestones contributed to their overall development?
>
> ➤ Reflect on your personal growth as a parent throughout this journey.

Building a Bright Future:

> ➤ Evaluate your efforts in encouraging lifelong learning for your child. What strategies have been particularly effective?
>
> ➤ Describe instances where fostering independence has led to positive outcomes.

Creating a Supportive Community:

> ➤ Share your experiences engaging in community events. How has community involvement positively impacted your family?
>
> ➤ Identify ongoing strategies for creating a supportive community for your child.

Conclusion

As we come to the end of this life-changing trip through the pages of this book, I sincerely hope that the story told in these chapters has sparked a significant shift in perspective in addition to providing information. The journey of raising children with Autism Spectrum Disorder (ASD) is unlike any other; it calls into question established beliefs and forces us to reconsider how we conceptualize neurodiversity.

Through exploring the complex fabric of autism, we have discovered the magnificence of its variety and the enormous potential that each person on the spectrum possesses. The chapters have provided windows into the lives of these incredible kids, with each page sharing tales of resiliency, successes, and the great talents that are frequently overlooked.

It is critical to understand that the diversity of autistic children's experiences represents a range of possibilities rather than a departure from a perceived norm. Their distinctions are individual reflections of the rich and varied human experience, not deficiencies. The overarching theme is one of celebration as we make our way through the complex terrain of early indicators, therapeutic interventions, and community engagement.

Every accomplishment, no matter how minor at first glance, is a victory. Every obstacle presents a chance for development. The tactics, inclusive communities, and support networks described in these pages are not only means of overcoming challenges but also of bringing to light the genius that every child on the spectrum possesses.

Let us, as readers, caretakers, educators, and advocates, come away from this investigation with a fresh understanding of each child with ASD—one that recognizes their innate worth and celebrates their strengths as well as their peculiarities. Let's create conditions where these kids' special gifts can blossom and the larger community acknowledges and appreciates the richness that autism adds to the human experience.

As we celebrate the range of options, we set out on a collaborative adventure to create a society in which "neurodiversity" is more than just an idea—it's a lived reality. We can all work together to create a society that is more compassionate and inclusive—one that not only accepts but actively celebrates the individuality of every child on the spectrum—by fostering an awareness, acceptance, and celebration of these differences.

I hope that this guide will serve as a call to action, an inspiration, and a catalyst for change. Let's work together to navigate this spectrum with compassion, knowledge, and a steadfast dedication to creating an environment in which every child—regardless of where they are on the spectrum—is valued for the unique person that they are.

Bonus Section

GUIDED REFLECTIVE JOURNAL

Date:

Milestones Achieved

Guardians Wellness Log

Water Tracker

Exercise Log

Long and Short term goals

1.

2.

3.

Long and Short term goals

1.

2.

3.

Things i am grateful for

1.

2.

3.

Monthly Check-Ins

1.

2.

3.

Notes and Reflections

GUIDED REFLECTIVE JOURNAL

Date:

Milestones Achieved

Guardians Wellness Log

Water Tracker

Exercise Log

Long and Short term goals

1.
2.
3.

Long and Short term goals

1.
2.
3.

Things i am grateful for

1.
2.
3.

Monthly Check-Ins

1.
2.
3.

Notes and Reflections

GUIDED REFLECTIVE JOURNAL

Date:

Milestones Achieved

Guardians Wellness Log

Water Tracker

Exercise Log

Long and Short term goals

1.
2.
3.

Long and Short term goals

1.
2.
3.

Things i am grateful for

1.
2.
3.

Monthly Check-Ins

1.
2.
3.

Notes and Reflections

GUIDED REFLECTIVE JOURNAL

Date:

Milestones Achieved

Guardians Wellness Log

Water Tracker

Exercise Log

Long and Short term goals

1.
2.
3.

Long and Short term goals

1.
2.
3.

Things i am grateful for

1.
2.
3.

Monthly Check-Ins

1.
2.
3.

Notes and Reflections

GUIDED REFLECTIVE JOURNAL

Date:

Milestones Achieved

Guardians Wellness Log

Water Tracker

Exercise Log

Long and Short term goals

1.

2.

3.

Long and Short term goals

1.

2.

3.

Things i am grateful for

1.

2.

3.

Monthly Check-Ins

1.

2.

3.

Notes and Reflections

GUIDED REFLECTIVE JOURNAL

Date:

Milestones Achieved

Guardians Wellness Log

Water Tracker

Exercise Log

Long and Short term goals

1.

2.

3.

Long and Short term goals

1.

2.

3.

Things i am grateful for

1.

2.

3.

Monthly Check-Ins

1.

2.

3.

Notes and Reflections

GUIDED REFLECTIVE JOURNAL

Date:

Milestones Achieved

Guardians Wellness Log

Water Tracker

Exercise Log

Long and Short term goals

1.

2.

3.

Long and Short term goals

1.

2.

3.

Things i am grateful for

1.

2.

3.

Monthly Check-Ins

1.

2.

3.

Notes and Reflections

GUIDED REFLECTIVE JOURNAL

Date:

Milestones Achieved

Guardians Wellness Log

Water Tracker

Exercise Log

Long and Short term goals

1.

2.

3.

Long and Short term goals

1.

2.

3.

Things i am grateful for

1.

2.

3.

Monthly Check-Ins

1.

2.

3.

Notes and Reflections

GUIDED REFLECTIVE JOURNAL

Date:

Milestones Achieved

Guardians Wellness Log

Water Tracker

Exercise Log

Long and Short term goals

1.

2.

3.

Long and Short term goals

1.

2.

3.

Things i am grateful for

1.

2.

3.

Monthly Check-Ins

1.

2.

3.

Notes and Reflections

GUIDED REFLECTIVE JOURNAL

Date:

Milestones Achieved

Guardians Wellness Log

Water Tracker

Exercise Log

Long and Short term goals

1.
2.
3.

Long and Short term goals

1.
2.
3.

Things i am grateful for

1.
2.
3.

Monthly Check-Ins

1.
2.
3.

Notes and Reflections

GUIDED REFLECTIVE JOURNAL

Date:

Milestones Achieved

Guardians Wellness Log

Water Tracker

Exercise Log

Long and Short term goals

1.

2.

3.

Long and Short term goals

1.

2.

3.

Things i am grateful for

1.

2.

3.

Monthly Check-Ins

1.

2.

3.

Notes and Reflections

GUIDED REFLECTIVE JOURNAL

Date:

Milestones Achieved

Guardians Wellness Log

Water Tracker

Exercise Log

Long and Short term goals

1.

2.

3.

Long and Short term goals

1.

2.

3.

Things i am grateful for

1.

2.

3.

Monthly Check-Ins

1.

2.

3.

Notes and Reflections

GUIDED REFLECTIVE JOURNAL

Date:

Milestones Achieved

Guardians Wellness Log

Water Tracker

Exercise Log

Long and Short term goals

1.

2.

3.

Long and Short term goals

1.

2.

3.

Things i am grateful for

1.

2.

3.

Monthly Check-Ins

1.

2.

3.

Notes and Reflections

GUIDED REFLECTIVE JOURNAL

Date:

Milestones Achieved

Guardians Wellness Log

Water Tracker

Exercise Log

Long and Short term goals

1.
2.
3.

Long and Short term goals

1.
2.
3.

Things i am grateful for

1.
2.
3.

Monthly Check-Ins

1.
2.
3.

Notes and Reflections

GUIDED REFLECTIVE JOURNAL

Date:

Milestones Achieved

Guardians Wellness Log

Water Tracker

Exercise Log

Long and Short term goals

1.
2.
3.

Long and Short term goals

1.
2.
3.

Things i am grateful for

1.
2.
3.

Monthly Check-Ins

1.
2.
3.

Notes and Reflections

GUIDED REFLECTIVE JOURNAL

Date:

Milestones Achieved

Guardians Wellness Log

Water Tracker

Exercise Log

Long and Short term goals

1.

2.

3.

Long and Short term goals

1.

2.

3.

Things i am grateful for

1.

2.

3.

Monthly Check-Ins

1.

2.

3.

Notes and Reflections

GUIDED REFLECTIVE JOURNAL

Date:

Milestones Achieved

Guardians Wellness Log

Water Tracker

Exercise Log

Long and Short term goals

1.
2.
3.

Long and Short term goals

1.
2.
3.

Things i am grateful for

1.
2.
3.

Monthly Check-Ins

1.
2.
3.

Notes and Reflections

GUIDED REFLECTIVE JOURNAL

Date:

Milestones Achieved

Guardians Wellness Log

Water Tracker

Exercise Log

Long and Short term goals

1.

2.

3.

Long and Short term goals

1.

2.

3.

Things i am grateful for

1.

2.

3.

Monthly Check-Ins

1.

2.

3.

Notes and Reflections

GUIDED REFLECTIVE JOURNAL

Date:

Milestones Achieved

Guardians Wellness Log

Water Tracker

Exercise Log

Long and Short term goals

1.

2.

3.

Long and Short term goals

1.

2.

3.

Things i am grateful for

1.

2.

3.

Monthly Check-Ins

1.

2.

3.

Notes and Reflections

GUIDED REFLECTIVE JOURNAL

Date:

Milestones Achieved

Guardians Wellness Log

Water Tracker

Exercise Log

Long and Short term goals

1.
2.
3.

Long and Short term goals

1.
2.
3.

Things i am grateful for

1.
2.
3.

Monthly Check-Ins

1.
2.
3.

Notes and Reflections

GUIDED REFLECTIVE JOURNAL

Date:

Milestones Achieved

Guardians Wellness Log

Water Tracker

Exercise Log

Long and Short term goals

1.

2.

3.

Long and Short term goals

1.

2.

3.

Things i am grateful for

1.

2.

3.

Monthly Check-Ins

1.

2.

3.

Notes and Reflections

146